# Substitute Teaching

*D.T. Gray*

iUniverse, Inc.
New York  Lincoln  Shanghai

# Substitute Teaching

iUniverse, Inc.

For information address:
iUniverse, Inc.
2021 Pine Lake Road, Suite 100
Lincoln, NE 68512
www.iuniverse.com

ISBN: 0-595-27558-3

Printed in the United States of America

# Substitute Teaching

# *Contents*

Foreword. . . . . . . . . . . . . . . . . . . . . . . . . . . . . . . . . . . vii

**CHAPTER 1**    First things First . . . . . . . . . . . . . . . . . . . 1

**CHAPTER 2**    Confidence . . . . . . . . . . . . . . . . . . . . . . . . 5

**CHAPTER 3**    Names. . . . . . . . . . . . . . . . . . . . . . . . . . . . 7

**CHAPTER 4**    Pluses and Minuses . . . . . . . . . . . . . . . . . . 11

**CHAPTER 5**    Knowing What You Teach . . . . . . . . . . . . . 15

**CHAPTER 6**    Bizarre Behavior . . . . . . . . . . . . . . . . . . . . 18

**CHAPTER 7**    Bad . . . . . . . . . . . . . . . . . . . . . . . . . . . . . 21

**CHAPTER 8**    Resources. . . . . . . . . . . . . . . . . . . . . . . . . 24

**CHAPTER 9**    Almost Whipped. . . . . . . . . . . . . . . . . . . . 29

**CHAPTER 10**   Corporeal Punishment. . . . . . . . . . . . . . . . 33

**CHAPTER 11**   Hall Passes. . . . . . . . . . . . . . . . . . . . . . . . 38

**CHAPTER 12**   Computers. . . . . . . . . . . . . . . . . . . . . . . . 42

**CHAPTER 13**   Subject Matter. . . . . . . . . . . . . . . . . . . . . 45

**CHAPTER 14**   Observation. . . . . . . . . . . . . . . . . . . . . . . 49

**CHAPTER 15**   Administration . . . . . . . . . . . . . . . . . . . . . 52

**CHAPTER 16**   Passing Periods . . . . . . . . . . . . . . . . . . . . 56

**CHAPTER 17**   A typical day . . . . . . . . . . . . . . . . . . . . . . 59

**CHAPTER 18**   Abuse by Children. . . . . . . . . . . . . . . . . . . 64

**CHAPTER 19** Last Bell . . . . . . . . . . . . . . . . . . . . . . . . . . . . . . . . 68

**CHAPTER 20** All As One . . . . . . . . . . . . . . . . . . . . . . . . . . . . . . . 70

# *Foreword*

No one wants to grow up to be a substitute teacher. I certainly didn't. But circumstances that I didn't seem to be able to control thrust me into this job several times during my career. At the first it was just a paycheck until I could find something else. I hated it. We were in the loose seventies and the students were rebelling like everyone else. Some of the classes I covered were just terrible. I didn't do a very good job then. I thought it impossible for a sub, that's what we're called, to control the hard classes. Even then, though, some of the classes were good. I couldn't figure out what made the difference. When I did have a full time teaching position I learned that many administrators consider the way the students behave for a sub as a reflection on their teacher. That is, if the teacher has control, the sub has an easier time. And I came to believe this somewhat. Somewhat, because everybody knows that when the cat is away the mice will play. But that's not an always situation either. Sometimes the best kids act up with a sub. Sometimes the worst kids do well with a sub. But in the last two years I have been really looking at this job called substitute teaching as I was doing it. There are many factors which come to the fore in such a position.

I will go over many of the things necessary to be a good substitute and to teach instead of baby sit. That is what I've been doing and trying to do the last two years: teach in these classroom situations which are not always conducive to learning. My grade for the last two years is 'B+'. I can't give myself an 'A' because admittedly some classes just don't do well even with my technique of teaching.

I developed a behavioral technique. I'll devote a chapter to it, my system is effective in bringing order. It solves the problem of how to reinforce 'good' behavior (and in so doing increase the frequency of it) when you don't know their names. Learning names is very difficult when you see different sets of students each hour and each day. In my first attempt to sub I gave up trying; consequently, I lost one of the best tools in controlling behavior: calling them by their names. Recently I have found I can learn several in the course of a class period. And I do this without really trying. It helps to know just a few names. When you call a student by his or her name when they are misbehaving it has a ripple effect. The others think you might know theirs. But I will go into this more later.

Today, another problem has arisen. In my history as a teacher and substitute teacher never have I had to face a situation as we all do now. It is possible that terrorists may strike our schools! Previously there were bomb threats, but these were always threats in my schools. And the ones making them, students most of the time, were certainly not professional enough to carry them out. Today, it is a harsh reality that they may not be just threats. Substitute teachers along with the regular teachers and all staff must deal with these emergency situations if they happen and prepare for them as if they were going to happen. I always carry a flashlight in my satchel. It can be very dark if a bomb goes off. You are responsible for getting all your students to a safe place! First thing I do when I go into a classroom is to check the evacuation route. This varies from classroom to classroom, and you need to know it. Also check what signal (long blasts, or short ones) go with what procedure, some schools use different warning sounds. You don't want to get caught not knowing in case it really happens. I plan for one student to lead the class out. This is important. A class that follows one student will go out orderly and not contribute to the chaos that may occur in these situations. Sometimes I assign a student to lead the class out at the first of the period and sometimes I wait until the practice drill occurs to pick someone. It gets it out of the way if you choose someone at the first, but in the course of a few minutes you can sometimes identify and choose a more reliable student, and this might be crucial in case of an emergency. You must choose someone, because you have to pull up the rear. That is the only way you're going to know that you got everyone out. We will see more in this line later.

In the booming nineties I built a cabin on the South Canadian River. At first it was to be a retreat for my wife and I in our retirement. We divorced and I found myself living in this cabin for two years. I discovered I was no Henry David Thoreau. I missed people. A friend told me the pay rate had increased for subs, and so to make some cash, and more to just have some human contact, I started doing it again. To my surprise I found that I actually like it at times. And most of the time I am really teaching, but it is still hard. When I discovered my plus and minus technique for controlling behavior it started getting really interesting. For the first time as a sub I am consistently winning in the game of who runs the class. It became teaching for me.

Now, I hear, in my district, they are going to start using volunteer people as subs to save money. If you're thinking about doing it as a volunteer or a paid employee go ahead, but after the first couple of weeks you might want to do some research on how to do it. You may lose big time at first, but don't give up. Subbing is a skill. Give yourself time to learn some of the fundamentals and tricks, and you'll never regret it. This is your opportunity to influence the world of tomorrow, to help some needy kids, to educate, and to grow yourself.

I didn't try to soften the examples of profanity in this booklet. I could have used just the letter and blanks, but I believe that if you are upset by seeing the curse words in print, you will really be upset when you hear them coming from the mouths of children. So I wrote them as they occurred. You may want to stop reading here if they offend you terribly or skip chapters 7, and 10. And you may be in a system; there still may be a few, where overt profanity seldom occurs.

My experience came from an inner-city system. I'm sure there are worse, in terms of student behavior, but most school districts will not have the extremes in discipline problems that I encountered. I believe that my approach and my techniques will be valid in any system. Kids are kids, in my book anyway, and you treat them as such no matter what comes out their mouths. You may find, as I have, that they become more and more alike when their noses are in a book and they are scribbling as rapidly as they can to finish an assignment in your class. And I have always felt that even though I am a substitute they are my classes for the day. Even as a sub, and even though many of the students will tell you differently, still consider it your class. It is only your class for a day or two, but still in that day or two learning is to occur. With this approach it will.

# 1

## *First things First*

Plan for your day. You will need to carry a satchel, a backpack, a bookbag or anything that will carry the supplies you may need for the day. A five-dollar satchel from a bargain store suits me. It is light and you can organize the things you will need, and perhaps the kids will notice that you come ready to teach. The things you will need to carry are some fundamental items, and some things that vary.

You need a working flashlight. God knows what may happen in the schools these days, so you need to be as prepared as you can be. If a bomb went off you might find yourself in a very dark situation. It might be in your classroom, it might be in the evacuation route your kids go through. Carry a flashlight. There are other things that would be helpful in such a situation, but you can't carry everything, so just carry the basics. A whistle is a handy tool. If you find yourself in a gym class a whistle is an excellent way to get their attention. On a playground it is good, and I have used mine in classrooms. It only cost a dollar and it is well worth it. In an emergency situation it might be the only way to be heard.

In your planning, you will have to decide what school supplies you want to carry. I have paper in a cheap notebook, and pencils and pens. I pick up pencils on the floor and the grounds. It not only helps me to supply the kids, but it gives my old bones some exercise in bending down and picking them up. Some teachers will say that the students need to take care of themselves. They know they need pencil and paper and they should bring them for themselves. I say, as a substitute, it's a whole lot easier if they all are working and not disrupting the others. I furnish supplies.

The other things in your bag will vary. When I find a good lesson plan in a classroom I keep a copy, run off a few, and have it for future use. You can't do this often because your bag would get so full you couldn't carry it. But a couple of lesson plans in the subject that you most often teach can be very helpful. You can write a list of vocabulary words for them to look up. In a lot of classrooms you will find dictionaries if nothing else. This is the most frequent reference you will find, so you're in good shape, if nothing else, to have them look up words. These kids are not experts in the basics or fundamentals of any subject. Having them do something basic such as looking up definitions can do nothing but help them in learning skills.

Sometimes there are emergencies with teachers and there will be no lesson plans. You need to prepare for such days and a word list to be defined can't go wrong. You might even use your creativity and make up a word list of common words that they can define without a dictionary. Make a group project out of it (although group projects are more noisy than individual work, they can be used in a pinch.) Let them dream up definitions from their imaginations if nothing else. There are many ways to do most things. It's up to you to direct the classes into those activities that are educational and ordered. Some lessons send the kids to banana land. Once I covered in an art class where paint was all over the floor, it would have been a good skating rink if I hadn't stopped the assignment a previous sub had started and called the custodian to clean up. That's just common sense. But common sense with a little formal training can take you far.

Math questions are good to carry. Once I had a teaching assistant correct me in front of the class. "They're not questions," she told me. "They're problems." I told her they're not problems if you can work them…. You will have stuff to put up with from assistants. They know the kids and some of them think they know everything. You, if you are certified, outrank them and can assert your rights. If you're not certified you have to just do your best with them leading. But let's go back to the starting idea of this paragraph. Anyone can write twenty or thirty math problems on a piece of paper and run off thirty copies. It can be useful in some situations. All kids need to know how to add, subtract, multiply and divide, and they need to know how to do these without calculators, and do it fast. Practice in this can't hurt them. Carry these worksheets and no one can fault you on such a review assignment. Don't pass out a sheet on calculus or advanced algebra. You might think that this will challenge them and keep them quiet, but it won't. They'll trash it on the floor in two minutes. But if it's something they can do, they might do it.

Kids ask for white out, staples, tissue, and other supplies constantly. I carry Cleanex sometimes. It stops them from asking me to go to the bathroom to blow their noses, and thus, stops them from bugging you for hall passes. You will have to decide on what to carry in regard to these items. Carrying these things has a dual purpose. First it keeps you out of the teachers things, looking for items and going through drawers (seldom do I go into a teacher's desk looking for something), and secondly it shows the kids that you are on top of the situation and some may think you actually care about them.

Last, take some things for yourself. Sometimes subbing is unbelievably boring and you have time to read or do your business, or whatever. Bring it with you and do it only when the classroom is in absolute order, or you're on a planning period. I used to always bring a newspaper to read, but I found that when I started reading, they started playing and scheming. Yes, scheming. Some of them dream up things to do to a substitute for fun. Someone told me you can sleep sometimes in the classroom, but I think this is a rather risky practice. I've seen a few (very few thankfully) who would tie your shoe laces together or something a lot worse if they thought they could get away with it. So don't pleasure read while you're supposed to be working. Working makes the day go much faster, and it's what you're there to do anyway.

I prepare for the day ahead of time, and I always try to be on time before first class starts. You first have to check the evacuation route when you go into the classroom. It's supposed to be posted in every classroom, but I have found some without it. Some teachers don't go by the rules, and sometimes kids tear them from the wall. They wad them up into paper balls and throw them. If there is not an evacuation plan in your classroom, look around, find the quickest, safest exit you can see. Or ask a student. Your "good" students can be invaluable in giving you information. They've been on fire drills, or tornado drills before, and they know where you're supposed to go. But get this information ahead of time. Don't depend on the kids in an emergency. But in planning, asking a student may be better in terms of getting plans in your mind ,than guessing. Planning your class evacuation, even briefly, sets it up for you. Students may know how to do it, so you find out ahead of time, tell them if it happens, and follow up the rear. But keep in control and manage the evacuations. Giving short emphatic rules, just when the buzzers sound, lets them know that you are in charge, and scream out if someone doesn't follow instructions. In these situations a loud voice can be helpful.

To stress this again, I try to plan for drills or emergencies. You will need one student to lead the class and you will follow up the rear. That is the only way you would be sure that you got them all to safety. Sometimes I pick a student at the beginning of class to lead. This brings up the thought of a possibly dangerous situation to the class which may upset the more sensitive, but it takes care of business early. Sometimes I don't mention it and watch the students for a responsible one to lead the class in case of the dreaded event. If it happens, select someone immediately when the buzzer goes off. (Be sure you know the sound signal for each emergency event.) Treat every drill as an emergency situation, unfortunately, you may be right someday. When an emergency sound is started immediately tell a student, her or him, to lead the class out. Give quick instructions where and how to go. "You will lead, others will follow, single file!" They usually don't go single file, but even if they crowd a little they will make it out to a safe place this way. Some schools have you shut doors when you leave and some don't. If it's not written on the evacuation plan or stated on the intercom just close your door as you go out. You're responsibility is to get your students to safety in an emergency, and you will do your best to do so, even if it means carrying one of them. Handicapped students can cause problems in evacuation that you just have to deal with. You can find a way to get their wheelchairs out or with developmentally delayed individuals have them walk out hand in hand, or, as I said before, carry one of them to safety; you will have the strength or can get the strength from some of your other students to do this. Plan these things when you observe the students in your room, and in case of an emergency do them. Having a job and an idea how to do it can keep you calm in these emergency situations; wait till you get home to fall apart.

There are many other things that you will have to prepare for at the beginning of the day, but emergency planning comes first. In regard to starting them on their lessons, there is an old saying about a "Bum's Rush" that I find effective. You give them a difficult lesson and you give them a good push in the first minute, and many times little shoves the rest of the day will get them, perhaps a little smarter, out the door when the last bell rings. These things are what you do first. The other things I will discuss in some detail in later chapters.

# 2

## *Confidence*

Your best tool, your best weapon, your best friend is your own confidence in yourself. People see it; students see it. It is apparent. With this on your side you can be a successful sub without much effort. Everyone has seen classrooms that fall from loud noise to silence when a teacher gets to the door. Everyone has seen classrooms that fall apart when the most well meaning person does his best to control the class. What is the difference? I think it is confidence. Some people seem to be born with it, while most of us have to earn it. But when it's there, people know it; students know it.

Don't be disheartened if you think you have none. It is something that can be won, and sometimes very quickly from a long term subbing experience. I didn't say it would be easy. In fact, it may be the hardest thing you've done in your life. But don't give up before you give it a good try.

Effective substituting involves getting all your stuff together. I mean most all your stuff. If you're just out for money, fine, but don't substitute teach; we have plenty of those in the system. But if you prefer more abstract goals, this may be your line of work. Whether it's philosophy, religion, morality, existentialism, Christianity, farming, family, parenthood, etc., whatever it is you're about then at least consider your philosophy of life before you sub. It helps if what you believe in is somewhere near the mainstream of society. Pedophiles and other sex fiends don't belong, or last long, in the public schools. If you're not certain of everything you believe in or are about, that may be better. You will have time and sometimes be forced to examine the things you believe in, and then put them to work. In other words you the substitute will be taught by your teaching experience, but you the substitute will do better if you know something of what you believe in before trying. I don't want to make this too hard. It is a matter of settling business with yourself that you've been putting off for years. All I'm saying is to just know you to some degree, and then try subbing and see what happens. So many times people do the same things, over and over, and make the same mistakes. They can't understand why life treats them so consistently bad. Make your mistakes, and then see what happens if you do things a little differently, then maybe more differently. I'm not suggesting that substitute teaching is some type of experimental situation for you to work on your own problems. I am saying that there are many ways to do things in this situation, and you will probably have to find the ways that work best for you.

No telling where you'll end up. The subbing experience and process, if you keep things directed to the teacher's lesson plans, will educate, to some degree, some kids in the process.

Keep to the teacher's lesson plans unless there are none. In that case you will have to make up your own. It's not hard. Almost all classrooms have textbooks and you just ask a student which one they're in and what page they're on, and you go from there. If you don't have a good base in education yourself, you will have a more difficult time, but no one knows it all anyway. Follow the plans. Plan to take care of your students first, plan for the day of teaching next, and then follow your plans.

You may be interrupted many times in following your plans, this happens even to the regular classroom teachers. Then you go with the flow and keep in mind what you will do in an emergency. They don't announce those. Just do your best.

Maybe I've overplayed confidence, certainly other factors gain respect from students. They are a curious mixture, these students. They like odd things. One guy may come to school on a motorcycle and they all love him. And an ex-marine, lets say a true hero, comes in and they hate him. They like different things at different times. I've seen petite old ladies teach circles around me, and I've seen veteran teachers not do as well. Sometimes these mystical elements, lets call them that, come and go and manifest themselves in odd ways. You know it when it happens; you feel it, but when you search inside yourself for a way to project them, sometimes they don't seem to be there. You won't find out about it until you try. And that is my advice to all: try.

# 3

## *Names*

Once I was in a staff meeting for psychologists mostly. There were other staff there, some secretaries, I don't remember all who were in the room, but I do remember that a new supervisor had been hired and we all had contact with him before, but this was the first staff meeting for him. In the meeting he knew all the therapists' names but mine. It was almost an insult. I got over it, but I've never forgotten it. Looking back, I'd have to say that I was probably one of the best in the room. I know it's difficult at first to get all the names, but when it is yours that is forgotten, you remember.

One of the most important things that you have is your name. Your parents gave it to you, and you use it all the time. You're the one who dictates how it's pronounced and sometimes spelled. When someone learns it quickly you notice. When someone repeatedly forgets it; you notice that too.

I couldn't pronounce a Vietnamese girl's name the other day. I was subbing and had tried several times to say her name, and she got very frustrated. Finally, I came close enough that she let me off the hook. That day I had small classes, eight or nine per period, and I got most of the names for the full day. Using them in class is very helpful. I've forgotten most of them now, but just for that day, it helped me to call a few students by their names. They worked hard for me that day, and I worked hard for them. Maybe we both learned something. You may stay in the same school for extended periods. In these cases it is feasible for you to learn a great many of their names. Start with the 'bad' ones and then put equal effort into learning the 'good' ones. It will pay off.

I tried to pick up a few names when I first started subbing, but it seemed such a daunting task for me that I just gave up for a time. This giving up meant that I could not call the 'bad' ones by name and write up a discipline referral if necessary. I also couldn't reward the good ones, by far the majority, who worked.

Once I had a parent who insisted on talking to me at school on the phone. It was on my planning period. I could hardly remember the name of her son, and putting his name with a body, even though the incident happened earlier in the day, was difficult. His was a minor infraction of the rules. I never guessed having her son write a few sentences would set a parent off so. Over half of that class had misbehaved badly, and I assigned them sentences to write; I probably should have sent a couple of them to the office. I don't think I did. I assigned the sentences to most in the room. It was a kind of blanket punishment for a class that deserved it. I really didn't expect to get any of my assignment turned in. I wrote about the incident to the teacher and told about the assignment I made, but didn't plan to follow up. When the principal asked me to take the phone late that day, I couldn't, not only, remember the name of the boy in question, I couldn't relate intelligently the sequence of events that led to her son's having to write a page of sentences. That parent raked me over the coals. I deserved it. I didn't think so at the time. After all, I was just a sub, and the whole class seemed to be acting up. Her son was guilty, for sure, but if I couldn't relate correctly the sequence of events that led to the behavior and the discipline, then it was me who should have written sentences. I couldn't see this logic at the time. I thought I was being mis-treated. First, by the principal who made me answer up to the parent, but also, by the lousy fate which put me in the role as substitute teacher to begin with. But for me, then, forgetting was a kind of blessing. I was having so many discipline prob-lems to deal with that I wanted to forget everything about school when I left the grounds, and so I did. It was only on this last time of subbing that I started to begin to catch some of their names, and remember the sequence of events that led to the infractions of rules. I've found it very helpful.

Emmanuelle got me out of a bad situation. A teaching assistant and I got into a confrontation in a learning disability class, and I lost my temper. This is after all the experience I've had in controlling my anger. I thought she put a wheel chair student, profoundly retarded, in improper restraints that impeded his breathing, and I let her know I was unhappy. I had rank, I am a certified substitute teacher and she is a teaching assistant, but she knew worlds more about this kid than I did, but I knew more about classroom management than she did. The assistant principal, who she called into the fray, determined that I should follow the teach-ing assistant's instructions. I assented, but thanks to a good substitute secretary, I was reassigned elsewhere for the rest of the day. But in this process of getting angry, which I strongly discourage, another student, supposedly retarded, guided me away from the confrontation. He asked me to test him on some easy words. I did and cooled down, and then was able to get myself together. I stated my case to the assistant principal in a logical manner. His determination went against my opinion, but I didn't argue. It wasn't helping these students to have dissension in their classroom. —This happened weeks ago. I do remember clearly the sequence of events that led to the problem, and I do remember that my behavior was justified, but still I lost, or was overruled. It would have been better if I hadn't let myself get angry. I was in the wrong for this, and the assistant principal was right and wrong. The teaching assistant had tenure in those classes even though I had rank. She had to deal with these difficult kids day in day out. I was just in there for a day. My angry behavior was unacceptable, even though I can justify it to myself by saying that I was scared for a child's safety. I was still out of order. She and the other assistant shouldn't have left me alone in that classroom with this special needs student, but it was I who blew my cool and started giving orders to her. I was wrong, she was wrong, the assistant principal was wrong and right in his determination. I shouldn't have let myself get angry in that class. That is my rule; it is a good rule, and I broke it. It would be better for me if I could learn not to get angry in a classroom, or to not let it show. Those special needs kids didn't need to see me arguing with their teacher. I handled the situation. I helped the kid at risk so he could breathe until the two of them came back from their break, and then together we readjusted him in his restraints and chair and he got all right. Even though I feared a life and death situation, I would have done better to have swallowed my fear and subsequent anger for a time and gone on. It became a power thing between the teaching assistant and me; it was silly, and I should have known better. —Such is substitute teaching. You can do better than my behavior that day. But I remember several names. I probably won't forget them, and still if something comes out of it in the future, which I don't think will happen, at least I will have some names for whatever reason. I , not only remember the names of both teaching assistants, the assistant principle and substitute secretary but also I remember the names of every kid in that classroom. Probably I won't ever need to use these names again, but, if I do, I'll be able to remember them. You will do the same. It is very rare that such an event as this happens, but you will remember names if it does.

Once, I had problems with my own name and students. My name is Mr. Gray to my students. In our society many students are obsessed with sex. In many different schools, I was referred to, by a few students, as "Mr. Gay." I don't know who started it. They thought it sounded clever I guess. Jokes go from one school to another faster than substitute teachers. My new name followed me. It was the sound of it. I don't know what else could have started it. It made me angry at first, I don't think I look or act gay, and the few who like to create disorder soon learned that they could use this false name to affect me, and they continued to use it when they wanted to set me off. And it used to do that very thing. Finally,

I found that if I ignored it, and then learned how to really ignore it, it took the fun out of it for them, and even if some continued to say it occasionally, they didn't get the reward of seeing me red faced and angry. Odd that it took a grown man so long to figure this out. I haven't been called "Mr. Gay" in a long time. There are things you can say back to these adolescent provocations. I may discuss a few later on, but ignoring, if you can do it, is a pretty good technique to use in most cases. What I've been called a lot lately in class, unsolicited, is 'sir.'

# 4

## *Pluses and Minuses*

It seems too simple to work. It sounds like one of those things the weird psychologists would tell you to do with your kid when she or he is misbehaving. It would be impossible to apply to substitute teaching because you don't know their names. How are you going to give them positive reinforcement if you can't write it down immediately? You will say, "I might try it sometime, but I don't think it will work, nothing works with these kids when they want to be bad. I may go ahead and read a little of this chapter, but I don't think I'll pay much attention to it, because I've tried other things suggested by psychologists and they didn't work so why would this…." False to all the above.

I had considered for a long time trying to develop something from my training to apply to the substitute teaching situation. I always gave up on these ideas because of the technical problems, mainly the name problem. How would one give reinforcement to twenty or thirty kids when you don't know their names. It occurred to me that you could use a seating chart, but I'd always had trouble using these. (They're only as good as the care the teacher takes in making them, and each teacher is different, and that makes the charts different. Some are good and useful, but others are hard to follow.) So, I did what I usually do and put the idea aside for a while.

While subbing in a difficult school something occurred to me. I had started using sign-in sheets to check role. Before, I had tried to call roll and had so much difficulty and made so many mistakes that I tried sign-ins and found that this method worked better. (When you call roll and mispronounce a name, which you are bound to do, laughter results. This laughter sets the stage for a party. You don't want a party atmosphere in your classroom.) Just have them sign their names. That way, I could cross check the roll sheet, look for forgeries, and get a more accurate reading. And this is important. The average daily attendance is how money is procured for the schools, and it needs to be done accurately, even by substitutes. From a sign in sheet the teacher, when they return, can see who was here and maybe find out who signed in for someone else. It is just a more effi-cient way to check roll. Later, I found, I also can have them put their student I.D.s. In this way I can weed out even more of the false signers. One could stand over each student while she or he signs, but you've got more pressing problems at the beginning of class. You have to attend to the learning of all the students at this crucial time, and I can't do this and monitor every signature. But in this hard classroom it was something else that occurred to me. I could get the few good stu-dents to sign a 'Good Behavior' sheet. Just put it down at their desks and have them sign it, at least those who weren't giving me trouble would get credit for it. I did and it had some effect in that class. Then this occurred to me, another use for a sign-in sheet…

This is a way I can deliver reinforcement to these students; I discovered. I have the sign in sheet in my hand. I can put it on the desk of any student. That stu-dent finds his own name, that he has signed, and gives himself a plus for doing work. Self-delivery of reinforcement is also superior to someone else giving it.

It worked the first time but not very well, for some reason only some of the students responded. It worked well enough, though, for me to think it out more. Then, later, in some classes it worked very well. And then it started working in even high school classes. I was excited. I refined it more, sometimes giving minuses for inappropriate behavior. In some classes this worked well also. Alto-gether I was getting some excellent results. So here it is:

First get their names on the sign-in sheet. "Get your name on the sign-in sheet, or you're not here," I say. "This is your assignment, and here it is on the board. (It's long and difficult enough to keep them busy for the time the period last. You may have to add to the regular teacher's assignment. (The students don't mind this, if they don't catch you doing it.) I say, "This is not a free day. You will be expected to work today." Sometimes I tell them about the 'conduct' grade I'm going to give them in the beginning, and sometimes I just start giving the ones who start working pluses. The later method gets their curiosity up. But after a while I tell them, "You will get a conduct grade today. It is based on how hard you work. You will get pluses for doing your work. Four pluses are an 'A'. Over four are an 'A' plus. (Some students will earn fifteen or sixteen.) To get them involved sometimes I have them tell me what three plusses are, what grade two plusses are, and what one plus is. And that gets some of them to accept it and get started.

I give pluses freely. With some students if they just open their book I give them a plus. And I furnish paper and pencils to those who don't have them. I don't want anyone in there who isn't capable of working. If some are not working, they can distract the others and pretty soon, if this isn't corrected, the method does not work. But still if there are only minor disturbances the others will usually keep working. If the disturbances are too big, or aimed at disrupting the procedure, I deal with them with regular discipline: warning, putting them in the hall, sending them to the office, or writing a referral. I do, in these cases, whatever the school and classroom procedure is. Getting them out when it is necessary keeps the others working, but what surprises me is that many of the typically disruptive students see this as an easy way to make a grade, and it is. Some of them have no experience making 'A's' and they latch onto the opportunity to make one. There may be other reasons these underachieving students get caught up in 'the game.' Every body likes to get pluses from someone and to learn a new game, but don't call it a game. It makes them devalue the procedure if they think it is just a game. (It is an evaluative procedure of appropriate work habits in a classroom.) A plus is a good sign, but with some you have to tell them this. "It's just doing what you're supposed to do anyway." I say.

A few minuses will sometimes be effective. For minor disturbances and to get some of the students started, a minus may work. If they get too many they tend to give up. Sometimes a student will make a slash on the sign-in sheet all the way across the page for his minus. I usually ignore this, and I have had students later, after earning some pluses, erase the big slash they made earlier. Also giving them a minus can start students who have earned several pluses go back to work. Minuses work well sometimes, but the pluses they give themselves are the big motivations. And the good students keep working for them after they have a guaranteed 'A +'.

It is a little distracting from their work to put the sign-in sheet in front of them and have them make a plus. It might detract the flow of learning in some students. But let me tell you, they don't complain. To have a quiet classroom, with a substitute, where they can think, is better than a few minor interruptions. And you can vary this. Sometimes I get a class started with some pluses, the class gets quiet, and then I tell them I will give two or three pluses at the end of the time block to those who finish and do well. That way I can sit down, and let them work independently for most of the time. If they start to get noisy, I get up and start giving pluses again. In some classes I'm on my feet the whole period, and in others I spend five or ten minutes with the procedure and that's all. This method is a tool you can use and modify to meet your personal preferences and the class needs.

Many times high schoolers, and sometimes middle or junior high school kids, will say this is like kindergarten. You can ignore it. Or you can tell them that all through their lives they will be evaluated in some way. Sometimes it will be on strengths and weaknesses, sometimes a scale from one to ten or to a hundred. But all of it, when boiled down, amounts to pluses and minuses. This is true and usually satisfies them; you keep up the delivery of reinforcers, and in most cases they accept it, and work for the reward of making pluses.

And that's about it. You can tally the pluses near the end of the time block and put a grade by their name, or if you're pinched for time, write on the sheet the grading scale for the regular teacher. They may decide to use the conduct grade or they may not. It doesn't really matter too much. You have accomplished your goal of keeping the class in order and on their task. You have won.

I have tried giving another reward with this method. Many students want to know who got the most pluses. You can just announce it. This pleases the winner. But after you use this method with the same individuals over several times, it sometimes is not as effective.

With middle school kids a piece of candy or a new pencil is something to work for. At times I have given such to the winner. This has not proved to be as successful as I hoped it would be. The poorer students, or the students who get minuses, tend to give up and not try for first place. The students who do their work all the time usually get the most pluses and the prize. But you may figure out a way to make this work. Yes, it can cost you a few cents, and some people think it's awful to have to pay kids to learn. But a few cents is something I gladly pay for a little peace and order in my classroom. And for yourself, you may find that if you are not dealing with discipline all hour, you start learning other effective ways to keep these kids in line.

With this method in my repertoire I go into almost any classroom with confidence now. (It's hard to use in gym classes and some music classrooms because of floor plans and seating.). But in most classrooms it works so well for me that I don't see how I ever got along without it. I have never had any overt objections to using it from the administration or parents. They see it working and they haven't objected to its use. Probably, as there always is, there are those who would object. I would let them, and probably keep using it. It has made the difference for me between chaos in some classes to an orderly pursuit of learning. Now it's yours if you want to try it.

# 5

## *Knowing What You Teach*

For a long time I thought my value as a substitute teacher was in my ability to answer questions that arose in class. In my district a certified sub teaches in all areas. That's right, all subject areas. To be able, then, to answer questions in all areas one must be pretty smart. I could tell myself that I would be like Sir Francis Bacon and say that all learning is my province—but it isn't. I can get though a Calculus class, but I don't answer questions about it, because I know absolutely nothing in that area.

One of the kids in the class will know Calculus. It is a matter of channeling the questions through the right individuals. Sometimes the right individuals don't feel like helping the jocks or preps or subs in the class. Then you have your work cut out for you.

The helpless approach sometimes works. The individual in the class who sees the sub trying but hopelessly failing may take pity on him or her and start helping.

It may not be necessary to ask for help. There's usually a book in front of you with step by step procedures for doing everything. Try to follow the steps. If you fail, perhaps one of the brainy kids will bail you out, and if they don't you might be surprised what you can figure out on your own. If you fail, the kids are probably not any worse off. They might get the wrong idea about 'variential equations' or something of the sort, but soon enough they're going to discover they are wrong, and that you taught them incorrectly. Then they will correct their mistake, and probably learn variance more deeply for the mistake, and just go on. If they never correct the mistake you lead them into making, then it probably won't matter, because they aren't heading for a career in mathematics anyway. You are important as a teacher in these classes for the right things you can do, but not nearly so important for the mistakes you will make on technical questions. Now how do you like those odds? You may help some kids by eliciting help from the brainy ones, or you may figure out a few things on you own and thus help a few.

If you make mistakes on technical questions, it probably won't hurt that much, because you're just a sub, and they don't expect much from you. So in this respect you can hardly lose.

It's hard to get through some music classes if you don't understand any music or play any kind of instrument. Although the teacher you cover for will probably underestimate your abilities and provide a lesson plan for dummies to teach. This may be a film. I hate films. There is almost nothing you can do but sit there and hope the kids are halfway watching. In recent times, when the film is somewhat educational, I have the students take notes, and give them pluses and minuses for that. It is a worthwhile exercise and is training for college. It's rather hard to pull off, but with some classes you can. With other classes a film is an excuse for them to talk to each other and do as they please, and there's little one can do about it.

I'll digress a little now and talk about films in general. You get quite a variety of them. With VCR's and TVs in almost every classroom the range of films you can show is vast. I've shown everything from "The Lowly Earthworm" to "The Blues Brothers." And that was an unedited version of The Blues Brothers with pretty blue language. I wouldn't recommend it even though it held the classes attention. You just have to go with the flow mostly on the film issue. If that's what the teacher has planned, you just watch it. You might ask a few questions about it afterward, and perhaps tie some things in to what they are studying. It's not hard for them to understand the irony of the "The Sinking of the Titanic." Everyone said it couldn't sink. And just a few words about a film can help them to analyze it, in some cases very shallowly, but, at least, be somewhat critical of what they see......I think the worst film I ever showed to a class was about water-falls of the world. It was a solid hour of pictures and sounds of waterfalls. Everyone in the class, it seemed anyway, needed to go to the restroom before that film was over, and that included me. I thought I must have crossed that teacher in some way for her to leave such a film for me to show. But desert films can get pretty dry, and some humor can arise from dull films in unexpected ways. You may amuse yourself with films, but I don't think they're very educational. The kids see enough TV. But you can't do anything about that. So start the VCR and kick back and go to the movies. If you're lucky you'll only have to watch the same film three or four times that day. I'd rather teach than show movies.

So this is the way you get by sometimes in subject areas you aren't well versed in. However, in some cases, fundamentals of the subject area will be the lesson plan and you will have the opportunity to expand your knowledge base. I probably would never have learned the meaning of 'adagio' or 'andante' if I hadn't subbed in a music class. Admittedly being in charge and learning at the same time are rather difficult, but some things rub off on you. You get through the day and you learn a couple of things. What other job can you say this for day after day.

You'll also find that there are worlds more to learn even about the subject areas that you are schooled in. The old saying that you don't learn it until you teach it is true. You will be asked questions that will send you to abstract dilemmas you never dreamed of before. You will search your past for a metaphor to make something a little less murky, for yourself as well as for your students. You will think about once understood concepts in ways that you never dreamed before. You may find that after some classes you think you know, you actually know less than before going in that day to teach. Sometimes going back to fundamentals is the only way to get through. But that's just teaching. When it's done right it's the hardest job in the world. I've worked in the oil fields of sweltering Oklahoma, factories in Michigan, freight docks in Kansas, and teaching makes me tired in ways that nothing else did. But some kinds of tired are not too bad. A short nap after school and a restful evening, and I'm ready for another classroom, teaching who knows what the next day.

If you are reluctant to substitute because of a lack of knowledge, don't let that hold you back. You certainly know a lot more than most of the kids you will teach. I am constantly amazed at their level of knowledge about many things. You will know enough to get through the subject areas. Ask questions, and let them look up the answers. The Socratic method of teaching is based on asking questions so that the student will begin to ask himself or herself questions. It is a good method I think. And you can easily phrase their questions into your questions. With a little practice you will be a regular Socrates. Give yourself a chance. You might like it.

# 6

## *Bizarre Behavior*

It's been threatened a thousand times when I refused a restroom pass, but it finally happened the other day. Someone urinated in the room. I didn't see him; he might not even have had to pull it out. With those baggy pants they wear he might have figured out a way do it without getting his pants wet, I don't know, anyway, it was there on the floor and he admitted doing it, and he cleaned it up. One wouldn't think that they would even mention such a thing. We wouldn't have in my day. We didn't want anyone to know that we had to do that sort of thing. But times change.

Students' asking to go to the restroom is something you need to get used to. I've seen academy award winning acts to show how badly they need to go, and I've turned down kids who couldn't wait. It is a problem because in some schools they adamantly forbid letting them go. Sometimes I do anyway, when I think they really need to. No sense in causing them the embarrassment of going on themselves, or the pain of holding it. It's hard to tell sometimes who really needs to go. It is something that boils down to smell at times. You will just have to decide for yourself. Once I carelessly told a boy to use the trash can in the room and just barely stopped him from doing it in front of the whole class. In one school a principal took the door off the boys restroom. You can see their feet from the hall when they are using it. I guess that slows it down to those who really need to go, but once the teachers' restroom was locked and I had to use that one. Rather embarrassing. Sometimes I say there can't be more than one emergency per class period and go by that. You will have to develop your own rules on this.

Violence sometimes occurs in a classroom. Once a teen-age girl chased a boy around and around the classroom with a pair of scissors. Murder was in her eyes. I don't remember exactly how I got the scissors away from her; they went around the room enough times to get tired, if I remember correctly, and her anger subsided. Another time I could not stop a girl from taunting a boy and insulting him, and when he finally blew, I couldn't stop him from going after her. She got up on the seat of a desk for some reason and when he pushed me out of the way he pushed her off that desk. She hit other desks and the floor; I feared her back would be broken, but she got up unharmed. Recently I broke up a fight in my classroom and got hit by an errant blow. That was the only time in all my substituting that I have been struck, and that was by accident. I didn't have to break up the fight. I could have just stood back and called the office, but I don't like that sort of thing in my classroom and I can stop them, so I do. I wouldn't advise anyone else to do it, my neck was sore for a couple of days and everyone thought I was wrong to step in. At least there wasn't blood all over the place in my classroom. But just the same, find out what school policy is on the matter and follow it. That is the best procedure on almost everything.

Sometimes bizarre behavior takes the form of verbal comments. In a good school the other day a boy in my class was chosen for student of the week. When they told him to go to the office to receive his award, he asked what he had blown up. In this time of terrorist attacks such a comment is inappropriate. I noticed the boy at other times in the day, and he was a child asking for help. A paper he turned in was covered with heavy marks and comments that were suggestive of excessive anger. Sitting near me at the lunchroom I heard him speak some questionable things to another student. If I had thought him a serious threat I would have reported him to the principal, but as it was I only wrote a note to his teacher. Letting it go through the chain of command is many times the best approach. I simply mentioned on my report what I observed and my opinion that the boy should go to counseling. I did also mention verbally, in more detail, what I had observed to another teacher who was familiar with him; she agreed. I do feel that this boy got some attention because of what I said and did that day, and that was without saying anything to the boy in question. I didn't want to violate the child's right to expression, but I felt, in this time period, he certainly needed someone to talk to him about the appropriateness of the things he said. Also, I hoped he would get some help with what I feared were problems of anger that needed attention. I attached the paper he turned in with the marks and comments to my report to the teacher. Sometimes you can feel viscerally when a child needs help. With this boy I had a little pain in my gut. I think my note to his teacher will result in him getting some attention.

In some schools you will be overwhelmed with feelings about many students. Many of them will behave bizarrely in your classroom. I won't go into extensive details: it will be anything from them rifling through the teachers desk while you are in the hall to openly fondling girls in class. It can be anything. What you do will depend on you. I find that I can't come close to correcting all the problems I see, so I focus on a few. Sometimes I don't get anything done, except making notes to a teacher whom I know is overburdened by behavior problems anyway. It would be nice if there were an easy place to separate these very badly misbehaving children. A place where proven techniques could be used to shape appropriate behavior, but, as far as I know, there are few of these places and the paper work and legwork to get children into them is very daunting. Some teachers, administrators, and parents will not take on the bureaucracy to place these kids. Consequently, many children who need special attention stay in the regular classroom. Among the behavior problems are the average kids. Both these groups are not getting what they deserve in terms of educational attention. The 'bad' ones demand all the teacher's time and the 'good' ones get shorted.

I won't sub in emotionally disturbed, E.D., classrooms. It may seem odd since I have background in psychology. It is just that I strongly believe that these classrooms do not belong with other public school classes. I subbed in one for a full semester once. But that was it. You may find that this is your cup of tea. It just wasn't for me. These classrooms will be as different as the children who occupy them. And they need help! I just couldn't give them much in the milieu that I found. I hated to see them at lunch with the other kids. They were always segregated in some way or the other, and they knew it. Better if their classrooms were away somewhere, I think.

You will see gross sickening things if you sub long enough, odd as the children can dream up. I'm talking about stomach revolting things such as grown kids sucking their thumbs or eating what they find in their noses. So be your own judge about this issue. And if you keep on you may not be sickened by anything you see. I won't give you any more details. You'll just have to see for yourself. And that's about it on bizarre behavior. You'll see it and you'll think it is bizarre, at least at first. But you'll see some ideal behavior too. It's up to you to decide what balances what out, or if you need to balance things at all. I do try to balance things, but that's just me. You will do it as you see fit.

# 7

## *Bad*

I don't know how to describe this, this situation you might find yourself in. Thankfully it is rare, even in the inner-city school systems, but it happens. It must be a combination of several factors: a teacher who can't control the students, a society and parents who can't control some of their kids, or a world where people have the propensity for going wild. Whatever causes it, you might find yourself in the role of someone who is supposed to manage it.

Sometimes you sense one of these classrooms. Teacher's desk in the corner, tables seeming to provide some type of barricade for the teacher, you will see this and the general mess, (even after the custodians have cleaned) that exists in this classroom. A look of barrenness may prevail. Maybe there will be a sad attempt to put something up for decoration, but this also might be torn from the walls. Objects that can be thrown are stashed away, things that might be used as weapons, absent. This is a war zone. You will be able to guess this before the kids come in, and if you haven't, it will take about a second after the bell to know it.

You might come in the room to find one of them at the teacher's desk, rifling through the drawers. Most will be standing, milling, and searching for the meanness they will pursue this day. They see you and start their routines.

It doesn't matter what they ask for. They are just feeling you out. If you let them go somewhere you're going to be easy. If you resist, you're only a little harder or challenging. They will try to overcome you, it's just a matter of a few tricks and a little time.

In these rare classrooms they are masters at diversion. First your orders are either completely ignored or obeyed in slow motion. But before you can follow up, there will be one of them asking or demanding attention for something else. Misdirection is their best weapon. They can shout for your attention, touch you inappropriately, say the most intimate things to you about your personal life, and do most anything to keep you from following up on any of the attempts you make to create order. It is chaos, nothing short. They make it, they hate it, but

21

they can't stop themselves. It feels like the twilight zone to walk into one of these classrooms.

About the only thing I try to do in such a situation is damage control. There will be a couple of innocents in these classes. I try to be where I can help them. And I call the office if it turns violent. You can go next door to other teachers and they may come in and scream at these kids for a time, but that effect doesn't last long. No one seems to know what to do with these students. They create the disorder, and hate it at the same time. The best I can do is step back, ignore their insults, and try to protect them from harming each other. One sub told me about a situation before Christmas. Someone had put up a tree for a class of these miscreants. An older man came in to sub, and, as they saw, gave up very soon on them. He simply sat at the desk and didn't say anything. Before the class was over they were breaking the Christmas tree ornaments over his head.

I try to bluff a little. Pretend I can do something to them, or would take the time to try. I guess I'm like everyone else in this situation, just glad to get out. Just leave them for the police. Thankfully, you don't see these classrooms often. When I was in college taking teacher training there were hints about such situations. One very prim looking young female teacher asked the class what they would do when a student told them to 'fuck themselves.' And there was a book that was required reading: The Lord of the Flies. I didn't really get the significance of this book for the classroom until years later. It does seem that there is an animal nature about us at times. If this is left unchecked it may rule out. I think that is what I see in these rare classrooms. It is a part of being human that resists being educated. It may be more natural than the three R's, but is really daunting to new teachers when they see it. Fortunately, most systems are winning against this primitive inclination. Most schools have order and you only see vestiges of the disorder in the better schools. I have great respect for the teachers who battle this hand to hand each day, and in some cases lose.

More often you see a type of chaos in gym class. Because of the nature of it there is less control. You will find accesses locked, it is hard to find a buzzer to contact the office when you need to, and there are so many of them to cause problems. You will probably have to wait for someone to come down and give them a basketball. They're afraid these kids will throw them at each other or steal them. Again, when I'm in this situation I do damage control mostly. I try to protect the weak, but one can not always do this. I make motions to stop fights; I scream loudly, send a student for help, but am mostly ineffective in this situation, besides blowing my whistle. Gym classes are usually very difficult to sub in. If you save the whistle for emergency situations, it is sometimes more effective.

Once I found a teenage girl in the boy's locker room. She was just sitting in front of the mirror making up her face. I had a difficult time making her leave, boys were gathering around her, and later when I got busy with something else, I found that she had gone back in there. This time I had to threaten to call the principal to get her out. What can you say about the dangers of such behavior? Anything could have happened in the seclusion of that locker room. This girl seemed to be interested in having more than one partner. Multiple sexual partners exponentially increase the odds of transmitting venereal diseases such as AIDS. This is not to mention the danger of violence in an unprotected area such as this. As a substitute you have to focus on what goes on in the gym. Heated basketball games often erupt into fights, so you can't be going into the locker room all the time to check on what goes on in there. I reported the girl's behavior to the principal and suggested she get counseling. There seemed to be nothing else I could do in the situation.

Like I said, you won't find happenings such as these every day. You will just have to do your best, you probably won't get much help in gym. Don't let it get to you when they absolutely ignore what you say and do. Learn from this. Ignoring their demands in a regular classroom can be a very effective tool for you to use. Learn from the miscreants and modify their approaches in a less difficult class, and you have another method to obtain control.

My technique of giving pluses and minuses is almost unworkable in a gym class. How do you reinforce them when they are running and jumping around all over the place? Occasionally I have given pluses to the ones who sit quietly in gym class, the effect does not transfer to the whole class because of the size of the gym and the multitude of stimuli that are going on. It may have some effect though, at least, you give attention to the kids who are not causing you trouble. Gym classes are difficult for subs, but just hang in there. The bell will eventually ring; the day will eventually end. Don't leave and go home even though you want to. Just keep your own sense of order within yourself and sometimes this affects them. Sometimes they settle themselves down. It would be better if they would assign two subs to gym classes, but they don't.

# 8

## *Resources*

Take advantage of all the help available. There will be other regular teachers nearby who can control most of these kids. Use them when you can. Unfortunately, they usually come into your classroom and shout at the kids and get them quite for a minute, and when they leave, the kids go back to what they had started. However, a minute of silence can help you regroup and try another tact.

An assistant principle taught me a great deal about teaching. It was in one of the 'bad schools.' I buzzed for help. There should be a working intercom in every classroom and you shouldn't hesitate to use it. It seemed the whole class was ignoring my shouts for order. This principal simply stood before the class, saying nothing, and desultorily, the class got quiet. In their vernacular she showed them how to 'chill out'. She stood there chilling herself and they slowly followed her lead. I started using this approach at times with some success. Some will try to throw you off by asking inane questions, but you keep your cool, and just stand there with a calm expression, and in some cases the class will cool down too.

Usually a principal or another teacher will come in and dress them down with a tirade: sometimes shaming them, sometimes insulting them, mostly threatening them. Again, this lasts about as long as it takes this person to get out of earshot. In many cases this has come from someone who just heard my loud classroom from the hall. They, trying to help me, came in and interrupted my procedure. It takes sometimes ten minutes for my pluses and minuses to take hold, and they made it longer. Their interruption made my system more difficult to work. This happens. But more often I have had other teachers and principals step into my classrooms with looks of disbelief at the quiet way the whole class works, after I get started.

As I said, if you need help don't hesitate to ask for it. You may find yourself not much better off for it, but at least it shows the kids that you are not afraid to buzz the office and this may prevent larger infractions from occurring. Sometimes help comes from unexpected sources. I have had custodians and maintenance men come into a classroom and without saying anything the class gets better. A parent in the room could also be positive. Someone who they are not sure about can make them be reluctant to pull some of the stuff they would with just a sub. Another overlooked resource in your classroom may be a student. Sometime, and I don't know how it happens, another student will have leadership abilities or great fear inspiring qualities. He or she will help you calm down a rowdy group. I wouldn't depend on this, but sometimes it happens, so just enjoy it when it does. This student later may ask for extra privileges and sometimes I let them leave for a while and take care of their personal business. This is if they've really helped. And, later, that student may cause you the most difficulty.

I know I am making this line of work sound really bad, and, even in the worst schools, sometimes it isn't. Most of the time classes are fairly orderly and are just boring to supervise. I have a friend who retired from teaching elementary and she does well substituting in secondary classrooms. She tells me she just tells them they can talk but not too loud, gives them the lesson and then sits back. Different people bring different dynamics into a classroom, and the kids respond in different ways. For me, at least, it seemed that they would try their worst behavior on me, and I had to deal with it. This is also the case with many other subs. I have talked to other substitutes who were just devastated by the behavior in their classes. Don't let it get to you because it really isn't personal. It may seem personal in the most personal kind of ways, but they forget you faster than a past holiday. Some of them have seen how classes can get out of control and they like to see if they can work this on you. Most are not happy when it does, but still they like to test you.

Another resource you have in your classroom is the textbooks. In most classrooms there are a few dictionaries. The kids don't particularly like to look up words, but if you get them started, it is something they can do. Something they can do is something they will do if you insist. I carry a word list. I just make up twenty words or more. I copy them off on twenty or thirty sheets of paper. There is a little expense involved but wouldn't you pay a few cents for some quiet and the ability to do your job better. Something about having an official looking sheet in front of them makes them think it is the real thing, and they will more likely look up the definitions this way than if you just write them on the board. This is something you can do quickly on the board, and that works in many cases. In general, though, they tend to not do assignments that they know the sub makes. Most of the time these assignments are not graded, unless you grade them yourself, and the students won't work as well for assignments that will not go on their grades. That is why I have work in my satchel. Many will assume it came from their teacher and will do the work.

Other books can be helpful. Any kind of a map can be a good class exercise. Kids, even high schoolers, like to draw. It is not too difficult for a student to look at the outline of a map and reproduce it approximately on a sheet of paper. Sometimes you can teach them how to do this. And many will enjoy and benefit from such an exercise. I carry some typing paper for this. It is more effective if they have a blank sheet to either trace, I let them do this, or copy a map. They have to fill in names of places. These may sink in if you tell them some of the important aspects of the places on a particular map. At present I think any of them can benefit from reproducing maps on the Middle East; their ignorance about geography never fails to amaze me.

Another exercise with maps can be useful at time. Some classrooms have the large, pull down, maps mounted on a wall. If you have a class that is fairly orderly, you can have them go to the map, two at a time, and let them compete to find places on it that you call out. The one who finds it first stays and another comes up to play. These kids are usually very competitive and they like games such as these, and these are games that have an educational payoff. The problem is if they get too competitive. You must have some order to do exercises such as this. If you do, the learning is cumulative and applies to other subjects. It is a good exercise.

Math competitions are also very good if done correctly. Just rattle off multiplication or addition problems, several of your students won't know their multiplication tables, so just say nine time nine, and have them raise their hand if they want to answer. Some will learn like this. You can do this with them in their seats and just being able to answer is reward for some. Or two can be called to the board to compete. The one who writes the answer first stays at the board the other sits down. Even in the so-called advanced classes, practice in the simple operations of multiplication, division, subtracting and even adding can be useful. Just use longer numbers and a calculator for your own benefit.

Sometimes I instruct a class on how to participate in an auction. I tell them they shouldn't give away their ignorance by counting on their fingers, or moving their lips in figuring. If they can figure correctly and quickly to themselves they will save themselves money. And I believe this is true. Any time you can justify an exercise by giving a concrete example of its benefits, do it. They can see the value of what they are learning when you give examples of this sort, and that has motivational importance.

There are countless exercises that you can develop in a classroom. First you must follow the teacher's lesson plans, but nothing stops you from expanding this at times. Your goal is to educate, and finding the exercises in which you are best able to do this will be most effective. If someone criticizes you for bringing your own material into his or her classroom, you might want to think about it, but I would continue in other classrooms. It sounds cliche'd but it doesn't hurt to come prepared.

Of course you are not there to indoctrinate. You may have many political, religious, or social opinions that are best kept to yourself. If you are instructing students in learning skills in various subjects, you won't be called up on it. Teach your students how to learn and let them arrive at their own opinions.

Someday I might meet with opposition to my plus and minus system. It is something new for some of the school systems to have a substitute come in and hold class. I would say that many times I get more work turned in than the regular teacher does, and such an event is not without some controversy. In one school, I have to call it a 'bad' one, a new set of guidelines came out during the year for substitutes. In it they stated that if you have a different or new approach to learning you must first clear it each day with the principal. Fine, but have you ever tried to say anything to a busy principal before the day begins, and what do they consider a new or different technique. I just go on at this school like I did before. I use my pluses and minuses and continue holding class. If they want to criticize me for it, then let them. The absolutely worse thing that could happen to me, that I could see, is that I won't get to substitute at that school any longer. Big whoopee. Oh, I don't know, there might be someone who says I shouldn't use psychological techniques (in the field my technique would go under the heading of theories of learning.) I believe enough teachers and principals have seen my approach work, and work well, that I would never be charged with any wrongdoing. I leave the sign-in sheet with the pluses and minuses for the classroom teacher each day and there is no attempt at hiding what I do. But even if something outlandish did come up I would have no trouble justifying it on a theoretical bases. Reinforcement has been an established principal of behavior, and in the schools for a very long time. I reinforce appropriate classroom behavior with pluses, and increase the effect by letting them record their own marks. This self-delivery of reinforcement has proven more effective than other means. Yes, I interrupt them for a second from their work to mark their pluses, but it seems to have no harmful effect on their learning. The alternative is for them to play the whole period, or, at least, do much less work.

There are many resources for a substitute teacher who wants to do his or her job. If you can get the classroom noise down you will be aware of even more. There are many acceptable activities for students. If all else fails have them draw their substitute teacher. This will motivate a great many of them.

# 9

## *Almost Whipped*

That was what I felt yesterday, almost whipped. I had five out of control classes back to back. I can't remember when it was so hard. It was in the 'bad' school, the one I go to for some odd reason, maybe because I think I can be of help there. I don't have to go there. I can go to the easy schools. But for some reason I respect the teachers there. It is hard, nothing but hard teaching those kids, and they face it every day. I have had success there with my method of pluses and minuses, but I didn't have, or at least at the time, think I was having any success yesterday.

Even in the inner-city schools there are ones that are harder than others are. It is the luck of the draw. There are no well-identified slums in my city anymore, but there are very poor areas. The kids from these areas are bussed around but some schools catch the brunt of their poverty. In these times the poor suffer and the kids of the poor suffer first. This seems the only explanation to me of the way this school is. The behavior of these children in the classroom is sometimes deplorable. They curse, they throw things, they push each other and they fight. That is just to themselves. The disrespect they show toward the substitute is sometimes profound. About the only thing they didn't do to me yesterday is attack me; I should feel lucky for this.

Even the principal, who I admire, got on my case yesterday. This is unusual. In first hour I called the office for help. I had a disruptive student who I couldn't identify. The student wouldn't give me his name and none of the other students volunteered it. I buzzed the office, which was my right and the principal buzzed back. He told me to follow procedure and write the student a referral. I'm sure the office was very busy, but I felt this was important too. I didn't have referral forms so I sent a student to the office for some. I wrote out the referral while at the same time the class went wild. It is asking a lot of a substitute to have all the information necessary to fill out one of these forms while he or she is teaching. Who remembers the school number, the student ID number, and other information requested on this form when you are going from school to school. It is difficult to just put down the date and time when so much confusion is happening all around. I find that it is best to avoid this type of paperwork all together. The time you spend filling it out is time where you could be on top of the on-going problems in the class. If the office would have just sent someone down (the student in question would not go to the office on his own) and taken him away somewhere, I wouldn't have felt the need to follow up. I just wanted him out of the class so I could deal with the other problems as they arose. As it was I lost the class. They were disorderly for the whole period. I did finally write out the referral on the boy and send it in. In the next class, by deciphering a poorly written seating chart and deducing the name, sent another one in. But in the process I lost the second class.

Almost exhausted after just two classes I decided I had to back off and just do fight and damage control. I stood in the doorway and let a lot of stuff get by. I only used my plus and minus method in two classes that day. In fact I made mistakes in using it with the first two classes.

When you have many severe behavior problems it is best not to use minuses at all. You start giving the minuses and the procedure becomes just another losing game for these kids. They lose interest very quickly, even if you offer a reward (I brought some candy to give the ones with the most pluses.) The 'bad' ones saw very early they didn't have a chance and disrupted the procedure for the whole class. In these classes just give pluses. In fact, it may be best to just give pluses all the time. I have had some success using minuses in classes where only one or two act badly, but it may have been better to just ignore these infractions and give only pluses.

In the classes yesterday where I used this method I got many more assignments turned in, but I didn't succeed in any of the classes in getting a work environment that was quiet and conducive to study. The lesson plan was too long, an open book quiz with about thirty-five problems, and many gave up before attempting it.

The lesson plan is important. If it is too short they finish too early and get noisy. If it is too long many give up without trying. With some practice you can estimate the appropriate length. Just add to it if necessary. It might upset the teacher if you changed her plan, but you can add to it, and in this way keep them working.

The room where all these problems occurred was decorated very nicely. Posters of several countries of the world lined the wall, and many encouraging phrases were posted. At the beginning of the day I felt there would be no problems with these classes. I always look around the room after I check the evacuation plan. It can give you some idea of what to expect. In a well-decorated room most times the classes are orderly. This didn't happen yesterday. It was tough all day long.

There is something that these kids use that I might elaborate on. It is a technique best described as disattention. A student misbehaves, and you are in the process of correcting him or her. Before you can finish with one another student demands your attention for something, usually something unnecessary. Yesterday a boy demanded to go to the restroom and wash his hand because he had touched a bandade on someone else's hand. This happened while I was dealing with a behavior problem of another student. I let him go (to shut him up) even though I thought there was no danger of infection. Some may interrupt you for a sore cuticle, a scrape on the ankle, an emergency bathroom pass, a drink, or in some cases a question about the assignment (in this case the question is asked not for information but to take your attention away from the disruptive student.) These come at times when you are dealing with a problem, and the questions are asked to divert your attention from the student in question. And they demand attention. It is difficult to ignore their interference and stay to the task at hand. When they distract you often enough, it is sometimes easier to just forget about discipline all together, and that is what they want. These kids have been dealing with substitute teachers since the beginning of their school. They have watched this technique work time and time again and they are masters in its use, and it usually works. So what does one do?

Ignore their demands and keep to the task at hand. It is hard to ignore a student who is screaming to go the rest room, but you have to keep on with what you started. You can cut what you're doing short. Tell the first offenders this is his first warning and then attend to the others, sometimes it is several, who demand your attention. But best, if you are giving pluses, ignore them all, and go to someone who is doing her assignment and give her a plus, then to someone else and give a plus. In these situations I give pluses sometimes if they are just sitting quietly. Sometimes the others who are demanding attention will get the idea that others are getting something that they aren't, and their jealousy will make them sit down and be quiet. It didn't work yesterday, but nothing seemed to work yesterday.

Finally at the near close of the day I felt some relief. I had made it through this hard day and it was about over. But then, without warning, two minutes before the bell, the class rushed for the door. In earlier times when I was younger and stronger I would stand in the door, especially on Fridays, and physically hold them back. This was a Thursday and I wasn't expecting it. They just got up and rushed the door! A boy was pushed into another and a fight broke out. They didn't stop fighting when I yelled at them, and I stepped in between them and shoved one away. I need to learn to stop this. I should have just let them fight like I have been told to do. They stopped though, the blood from one of their noses got on my new sweater, but they stopped. In addition, one boy who wasn't involved in the fight came up to one of the fighters and wanted to fight him. He had hit one of his friends. I had to deal with this character. The crush of the other students subsided as they got through the door and into the hall. I had to stay late to write referrals on the fighters.

And so the day ended. Going home and dealing with it all took me longer than usual. What happens to children like these? Does one just mark them off to a life of crime? Is there a possibility of setting up intermediate facilities (easy prisons I was thinking last night) for them to get some type of rehabilitation. I don't know, it is plain to see that the schools are taxed to the limits in trying to control them. I'm sure most of their parents have thrown up their hand and if not in person, psychologically abandoned some of them. I don't know. I can't just leave such alone. I have to go over many things until sleep comes and then the next morning I am ready to go again, but to the easier schools for a while.

# 10

## *Corporeal Punishment*

I once overhead a substitute teacher say that he did not know if he believed in corporeal punishment when he started substitute teaching, but after one week he believed in capital punishment. It is something, corporeal punishment, that does cross your mind at times. After all it was the method of choice in disciplining children for over three thousand years. It is just in the last three or four decades that we decided that it is harmful and promotes violence, and the general public has agreed. In practically all public schools in America it has been banned. In my early school days it was practiced liberally.

I saw a couple of beatings in my junior high classrooms. In one a boy was whipped with a board. The oak board broke on his bottom and he yelled loudly in pain. In another my cousin was caught eating candy in class. (In my classrooms at times I would let them eat lunch if they would do so quietly.) The teacher withdrew his belt and lashed him several times. Bruising resulted and my uncle went to see this teacher and gave him what for, but it didn't stop him from whipping kids. Both these beating were done in front of the class. I received a couple of spankings for silly things: not keeping my big mouth shut mostly. They hurt even though they didn't compare to the two mentioned above. I didn't cry, but I felt like it, and I was afraid that if I got one like my cousin had, I would cry, and that would be worse than the physical pain. To cry then was to be disgraced in the school. Neither of the boys cried that I mentioned. My cousin was always as tough as a nut. I didn't know if I could be so brave, so I curtailed my smart remarks, at least for a time, and tried to go by the teacher's rules.

Today, as a substitute, I see violations that are ten times worse than anything I saw as a boy. And most of these are let pass. It is a sign of our times and if you agree with it or not it is the law. You must obey it as a substitute teacher. You don't touch the children. As much as you would like to wring their necks, you don't touch the children. You can go through with the lengthy procedures of warnings and writing referrals if you think it is worth it, you can ignore some of it and go on, or you can use other methods.

I had a student shout out, "motherfucker," in class the other day. It just hit me wrong and I wrote him a referral. First it was a major problem getting his name. He went into ultra-slow motion mode and delayed telling me his name for some minutes. Then I was not sure it was his name. I looked at the seating chart. It was not orientated to the arrangement of the desks, but after calling out a few names I was able to ascertain the name that was supposed to be associated with the desk he was in. With this I was able to write the referral. I could have asked other students what his name was, but usually no one will tell, and the few who might volunteer would be putting themselves in some danger from doing so. Some of these kids don't let informers pass easily. A volunteer might meet with violence in the hall, so I usually don't ask other students to tell me violator's names. Getting his name and figuring out the school code and other information that was called for on the form kept me busy for several minutes. Finally, I had the referral written and sent the student to the assistant-principal for discipline. At the end of that class the vulgar perpetrator was back in the classroom, still creating noise and disturbance and I don't think anything was done to him for his breach of decorum in my class. Go figure.

I had other problems with this assistant-principal. Once, a learning disabled girl came to me in the hall and told me a boy had 'touched her'. She pointed him out to me and I motioned for him to come to me. He ignored and started giving me stuff like I had no right to even talk with him. I went to him. He started to back away and run. It so happened that I had a planning coming up and was determined to bring this boy to justice. He started to run and I told him he better run fast because I was right behind him. For some reason that stopped him. I was about to grab his arm and take him to justice when this assistant- principal appeared. I told him what the girl had told me, and the assistant- principal just nodded like it was nothing. He did take the boy into his office. I probably should have taken the time to find out the boy's name and written him a referral, but it just seemed that telling the assistant- principal should be enough. I don't know what happened to the boy, probably nothing. When the people in authority want to ignore everything, there seems little that a substitute can do. You will have to balance things and figure out what you will do. I could have gone through the school secretary and gotten the boys home phone and called his parent or guardian. I could have even driven to the boy's home and presented the facts to whomever I found there. I didn't. Maybe I should have.

Another thing that causes problems in writing referrals is the name the student gives you. It seems that many students have several names. I once asked a boy how many aliases he had. He finally gave me what he said was his school name and I wrote him a referral. The time all this business takes, steals time away from what you are able to give the class as a whole. In these classrooms you need to stay on top of everything or the class may be lost to chaos in nothing flat. I've had these chaotic classrooms and they are nothing to take lightly.

First, the word gets around. You lose one class and then the rest of the day other students will challenge you for the disorder you allowed in the other class. Sometimes they remember it from day to day. It does seem much easier to carry a paddle or ruler and whack them a time or two and just be done with it. But that is not the system now, and that is not the way of the country. If a substitute decided to do such as this, he would probably find himself on the evening news. If the slightest of bruises came from the 'beating' then a lawsuit would most likely ensue.

I suppose in the parochial schools and some private schools corporeal punishment is still used. It is a concrete type of punishment. It fits into the concrete way of thinking that most of these kids utilize. They are used to dozens of warnings and threats. Some teachers are so convincing at this that they get results. Their voices take on fiendish qualities, their faces burn red and they look like they will explode as they tell these kids they have to be quiet. But some do this and they still aren't quiet. These kids get lecture after lecture. The abstract quality of these lectures just doesn't seem to sink in. They are thinking concretely and they are being lectured abstractly and many of them don't hear a word said to them. They take the queue, and nod yes at some points and are let out on the world again to wreak their brand of misbehavior and havoc. So, what do you do?

I try to outsmart them, but at times they miss the point. Most of them have little intellectual depth and an insult will usually go over their heads. Once a young girl, bright looking, well dressed, and in every way looking like a good student, stopped me while I was writing a list of activities for them on the board. She asked if she had to do the problems in order. If she had to do 1,2,3, or if she could do 5,1,3, etc. and turn them in like that. Something about it struck me the wrong way. I could see the classroom teacher taking extra time jumping from one item to another on her page and trying to figure out if she had covered everything on the assignment rather than by just looking 1,2,3 for the answers. I told the girl that was a very 'curious' question. I guess it was the way I said it. The girl immediately became upset and accused me of calling her stupid. I have had that same girl in classes thereafter and each time she reminds me of the time I called her 'stupid.' I have come close to calling a student stupid. Going over and over a concept that is dirt easy on the board I've had student ask me to explain what I said over and over. It is frustrating and I've made replies that were not exactly appropriate, but never have I called a student 'stupid.'

Once, I asked such a repeated questioner if he could tell when school was out. He replied, "Yes, when the last bell rings." I amplified a little and told him it was also when all the children went home or to their various after school activities, and then I told him if he could figure that out, he could figure out what I had just said and put on the board. I don't know if my sarcasm was effective, probably not. But the best I've found is to keep them so busy that they don't have time to talk to you about the mindlessness that goes on with some of them. Maybe I'm getting old, but I don't argue with them any more.

I start with a good assignment. Something not too long or too short. Something they can do if they try. Then I employ a technique once referred to as the "Bum's Rush." I push them hard in the first minute of class. Give them their assignment, tell them I will give them a conduct grade for the day (obtained from my plus and minus system), start giving those who start working pluses and extol them to start now or they will miss the boat. If they do in fact start, and you will be surprised in how many classes they all do start working, I give them little pushes through the hour in terms of more pluses and more verbal urgings for them to keep working. The 'Bum's Rush' has worked many times for me. It is only in the very disruptive classes that the sequence can be destroyed and it doesn't work, but you will be surprised and delighted in the number of classes in which it does. You may even have some minutes to sit back and enjoy the quiet.

It is somewhat distracting to put the sign-in sheet in front of them and they stop working to give themselves pluses, but ask them if they mind. I've only had one or two tell me they didn't want pluses, and they usually recanted before the hour was up. Most say they like the pluses, and by the looks on their faces you can tell that they love to give themselves credit for doing what they're supposed to do anyway. And it can be rewarding when you recognize the behavior problem kids are deep in their books trying to earn pluses. One boy who I knew as a disrupter of classes asked me how to summarize a chapter, the assignment. I knew the boy was developmentally disabled. I told him and showed him how to write the first sentence of each paragraph, and told him that was one way to do it. The boy didn't take his head up from the book the whole period, getting many pluses. He turned in three pages of summary at the end of this hour. That boy hadn't turned in three pages in his whole student career.

So, it seems simpler to just whack them, but there are ways to get around it. You may frighten some by screaming at them. You may insult some into silence. Or you can outsmart them and trick them into doing what they are supposed to be doing anyway. I tally up the plusses, when I have time, and give credit to those who worked. Usually I say four pluses equal an 'A' in conduct. I have students who earn sixteen or seventeen in a single class, and in most classes they all earn an 'A'. This is something some of them have never earned. It is nice when you can give an 'A' to all the students in your class.

# 11

## *Hall Passes*

I've seen academy award winning performances of needing to pee. Kids are not bashful about it these days. Bathroom behavior is openly discussed in front of the class. Quite a change from my day; we didn't even admit to going. But mostly, today, it is getting out of class they want, a game.

It is a game that many students play. They see if they can get a pass from the substitute. Some schools give you written instructions to not give hall passes. Sometimes I read these to the class at the first. It may stop some from asking. But what I consider is that there are some who really need to go. Among the nervous ones, and there are many these days, going to the bathroom can be an immediate and strong need.

I try to separate the real from the phony. It is difficult, and when you let one go you have half the class who try to follow. Yet, to hold someone who really needs to go seems to me torturous. I had a boy once who wanted to go, he seemed to be honest and really in need, but instructions were to not let anyone go. In a few minutes he came back up. I smelled him and let him go. It, especially, for the upper grades would be a tremendous embarrassment to evacuate on themselves. So I go against orders sometimes. I don't have the authority to do so. I could get into trouble myself, but I still let them go if I think it is an emergency. I tell the others who follow with requests that only one emergency happens in a class period. But, if I think there is another I let them go too.

Once a boy told me he would pee in the trash can if I didn't let him go. I said for him to go ahead. I barely stopped him before he pulled it out. That stuff is just for attention. I didn't let him go after that. You just develop a sense about it. If the school does not say anything I take a liberal policy toward it. I don't care if they're out of the class for a few minutes. But it matters because in some schools they wander the halls and in some cases walk into other classes and talk to their friends. The bathroom problem is something that takes up time and is irritating. Knowing it is a game with some of them makes it more irritating; to have to stop and write a pass or just to deal with their demandingness is bothersome, but that is a part of subbing. I don't have hard and fast rules. I play it by ear, trying to recognize the ones who really need to go, and quickly dismissing those who don't. It's not easy.

There are also those who want passes for other reasons. A counselor visit comes up often. I listen and decide. There are those who have real schedule problems and need to resolve them. There are those who have issues that need to be addressed. There are those who need to spend the whole day in therapy with the counselor. I try to decide, with do attention to school policy on the matter. If there are not mandates against it, sometimes I let them go. Sometimes I make them do their assignment first and let them go as something of a reward. Usually I make them write their own hall passes. "Date, time, reason," I tell them, and they do the paperwork. I just sign. It is an area you will have to deal with; admittedly, I tend to be easy in this regard. I think the school counselors need to take a more active role in dealing with these kids, but they have mountains of paperwork anyway. I see so many who need some counseling that I tend to let them go when they ask, if they make a good case for it, but you will have to decide for yourself. I've had students write hall passes for themselves and two of their friends to go to the counselor. Of course these I tear up. But if they are legitimate in appearance I let them go until someone tells me not to.

Menstruation is another problem. In high school I remember a girl who spent half a time block with a bloodstain on her white pants. It was a terrible embarrassment for her. Today, most girls prepare for this, but some will need to go to the restroom. Let them go. Ask them if it is something female or something like that, and if they say yes let them go. I also have had pregnant girls who need to go to the restroom more because of their pregnancy. Let them go. There are many situations where you will have to just let them go. Sometimes I tell a student to wait a few minutes. In this time some will forget about it, and the ones who don't probably really need to go. So evaluate and decide and don't worry. Just observe and you will see the obvious fakers.

Going to the nurse is another thing. You will have something as minor as a hangnail or major as a serious disease. Look at the wounds they show you. If they look bad send them. Some students will allow you to put your hand on their foreheads. If they seem to have fever send them. Being sick is something you are not qualified to diagnose, but, here again, you will have so many who fake sickness that you will need to make some kind of informed decision or they will go in mass to the nurse. Once I had a girl ask me for some Tylenol that her teacher kept in the desk. I absolutely refused. I'm not about to administer any kind of medication to these kids. She sat down and began crying and then later acted like she was dying. She was faking it, but I sent her to the nurse anyway. There are legal things to consider in what you do, better to send someone who doesn't need it than to keep someone who does.

The illness situation is probably the most important. If a student is truly sick you don't want to stand in the way of their treatment. The bathroom situation could also cause you legal problems. It is remote, but if a student is incontinent in class and you have refused to let them go, a lawsuit might be pursued. Here again, the risk is so low you would probably not even need to consider it, but it could happen. This is what I evaluate and consider when I get a rule from the substitute secretary or the administration that no hall passes will be given. I've given hall passes in spite of these injunctions and haven't gotten into any trouble, but I take the responsibility on myself, and if you let them go you will too.

A regular teacher has so much advantage over a sub in these situations. They learn the kids very quickly and the kids don't try so much with them. Also, they have talked to the parents and in cases of medical necessity they know what to do. Teachers should leave subs notes on the serious medical problems of their students but they don't. You will be pretty much on your own in much of this. Listen to the kids, not only the one in question but the other students. Sometimes they will say something if a student has a problem. Just use your best judgment in these cases. If you make a mistake chances are it won't be a problem.

Passes to the library and to another class are sometimes requested. Usually I have them show me a note from the teacher on these, but sometimes if they finish their assignment in my class and there are no instructions to the contrary I let one or two students go. It is not a good idea to send your whole class somewhere else no matter how attractive the idea may seem. Have them do their work in your class and then use your judgment about the going elsewhere.

Hall passes are a problem. One of the things that upsets me the most is when a student is wandering the halls and comes into my class and starts talking to one of his friends. This was unheard of in my time. And it is very difficult to deal with. If you immediately buzz the office he will leave, and it is unlikely he will be caught. You don't know his name and probably can't get his name from the others. I've almost bodily thrown some of these out of my class, but I'm glad I didn't. It is just one high school where this happens at times. Most schools are ordered in a way that it doesn't happen. Kids will do things like this. Someone gets the idea and they do it when they can get away with it. This more than anything gets me though. It's enough to have the students in my class to deal with without having to deal with someone who comes in while roaming the halls.

There are many things to consider in giving hall passes. I certainly don't want to contribute to this problem, so I'm more severe about giving the passes in this school. In most cases I consider a hall pass as something of a privilege that has to be thought about critically before given. There may be repercussions in either way you go about them. Use your best judgment in giving these hall passes.

# 12

## *Computers*

Computers: the key to education or the bane to the substitute teacher. Computers have their special considerations. You will find one in almost every one of your classrooms today. My advice is to leave them alone unless you have instructions to the contrary. Once I was instructed to pull up lesson plans on one. I did so and immediately the thing went out of whack. I don't think I did it, but it was broken. Since that time I have been reluctant to touch one that belongs to someone else.

Sometimes there is a room full of them and your lesson plans are for the kids to use them. Go ahead. The kids know how to work them, but you better get ready for a day of walking. You will need to go from one to another to make sure the kids have not pulled up some sort of game to play instead of the assignment. You will need to check them all frequently because there are other things they shouldn't be pulling up. Pornography, if the machines are on the Internet, is very easy to access. This has a special appeal to the adolescent male and they can be very deceptive in bringing it on the screen, and switching it off, if you get within viewing distance. Be warned.

I guess I'm a little skeptical of computers. Even though I write on one and after having used a typewriter for years I have to admit it is so much better. It is nothing less than amazing that finished copy that can be printed so quickly. But the word processor is my primary tool. I use the Internet some, but I still go to the library for most of my research. I can't justify the extra time it takes except that information too easily attained may not be good information. It seems that good information needs to be given adequate time to be integrated, and I feel it is done better in a library than on the Internet. Maybe not, but I'm also afraid I might not be as critical of this easy information as I might need to be if it comes too easily. Just an old man probably, the kids are going to do it this way, and nothing I say is going to stop it.

I try to help them by being critical of some of the information they pull up in class. I do this because I see things on the monitor that I disagree with, and other things that I think are outright lies. Especially in the areas of the social sciences many of the things listed as facts are really opinions or based on research that is not conclusive. If you read what the kids are reading you will see some of this; there might be a great many things you will want to challenge. Sometimes statistically they can make a good case for their assertions, but I'm still not sure. You might challenge these things to your students and teach them to be a little critical of the information they tend to take so readily as fact. No matter how you look at it your day supervising a room full of students at computers is going to give you plenty of exercise.

Usually these classes are orderly. The kids are glued to the screens and few ask you for hall passes and few give you the problems you see in the traditional classroom. If you want to you can kick back and read the newspaper, but I wouldn't advise it. As I mentioned earlier they can and will pull up things that are questionable. Someone will come in (there always is someone who will check to see if they are breaking the equipment). They can see things that potentially could cause you some headaches.

I think computer time is best when it is integrated into classical type instruction. Too often we throw out the baby with the bath water. Regular classroom instruction has value. If it didn't it wouldn't have lasted for so long. These kids sometimes overlook some of the simple truths for the ready answers the computer provides. In many of these classes I ask the students where their best computer is. They usually point to one machine or the other. Of course, I am referring to that one which sits on their shoulders. Things can happen to the machines. What happens if a virus hits them? What happens if the electricity goes off?

I'm not a fatalist or survivalist, but sometimes, in small ways, these things happen. I wonder what will happen if they occur in larger ways. In classrooms, discussions come up that give students information as to how to survive in extreme situations.

Fall out shelters came up one day. Most of the kids thought they were absurd, that if there were nuclear war we all would be dead instantly. I don't think this is the case as it might have been earlier in the cold war. If there were limited nuclear war many would survive and taking cover for a while could be an advantage. Making some preparations such as having water set back could be a lifesaver if the water to the faucet was shut off for a few days. Having your pantry stocked with canned goods could keep you from going hungry until emergency food was provided. In so many cases that I see people tend to think in absolutes: either, ors, all or nothings, and in so many situations I see there are degrees. Degrees of everything are the way I see things. Just a little preparation for disasters can alleviate much suffering, and what difference does it make. It just takes a little time to draw your camping containers full of water. It just takes a few more dollars to stock your cabinets. If the emergencies are not completely destructive such measures could save you a lot of suffering. Well, I've gotten way off of computers. But I feel technology, while a great thing, is peripheral to the basics of survival. The kids need to know there are ways of getting by that existed long before their computers came on the scene. There are many ways of getting by if shortages occur, and the students need some instructions on these methods, but I don't feel it is my place to actively educate them on these things. Sometimes in discussion I will mention things, but usually the lesson plans points you in directions that as a substitute you must follow. It doesn't hurt to say that people can get by on very little if they have to when discussing a piece of literature that invites such a statement. To get into basics of survivalism is beyond the scope of the lessons most subs are expected to teach.

I wish in the "bad" schools there were some way I could stop some things. Specifically I would stop the rush to the door when the last bell rings. I had this the other day and it upset me. It happens sometimes, usually on a Friday when they are in a hurry for weekend. They just push and rush to get out of the classroom. In the news recently we heard of emergencies in nightclubs when panic took over and they pushed people down and many were crushed or were overcome by smoke. These kids need some severe penalties when they push to the door, and behave as a mob. Such behavior needs to be addressed specifically and the dangers pointed out. They don't pull up such information on their computers. They could read about the instances where it happened recently, but I fear they don't make the connections with their own behavior. Well, perhaps I'm getting old, and I should let them be, but if they were instructed on the dangers and follow up occurred the next Monday morning, they could learn to pass from the room orderly.

# 13

## *Subject Matter*

Most of the things I've talked about are related to the business of teaching in a situation where you are a stranger. This type of teaching is by definition difficult. But you learn to prepare quickly and react positively and you do okay. But to really do well you need some expertise in a subject area. You may say that you have a degree in a subject and therefore are an expert, but I say you just began to learn about your subject area in college.

In the day to day challenge of teaching you learn your subject thoroughly. Rules that you accepted as fact will be challenged by students and in some cases they put up a good argument. You will think about things and go deeper into your understanding and then you will truly become an expert in your field. In a class I was asked what part of speech the simple word "there" was classified in. I couldn't come up with an answer at first. I checked a dictionary and discovered that it could be used in four different ways and in each considered a different part of speech. It can be used as a noun, pronoun, adjective, and adverb. Such are the details you learn while teaching or even while substitute teaching if you keep your mind open.

In a learning disability class the assignment was word etiology. I happened to have some base in the area and quickly found the dictionaries that the kids could use. Many school dictionaries do not include word origins and other information about the use of words. I selected the dictionaries the students could use and went about explaining the abbreviations: ME equal Middle English, F equals French, LL. equal Latin, and so forth. These kids were far from dummies. Most had dyslexia problems. One girl wore thick glasses and had to position herself low and to the side of her book to read, but was very intelligent. That was evident from the questions she asked about the assignment. The lesson plan was good; just hard enough to keep them striving, and I feel they learned a great deal of how to find the origins of words that day. One student asked me how I knew this information. It was like a sub was supposed to be stupid. This student couldn't figure out how I was privy to such technical information. I simply told him that I went to college. It seemed that for the first time he saw going to college as a benefit for anything besides getting a degree and a high paying job. That was a very good day. In all classes they worked and learned. In one instance a very reserved black girl needed help with the lesson but wouldn't ask; I sat beside her and we worked out some of her lesson. Another teacher was there; she had another class in the same room. She said that was the first time she had seen that girl let anyone help her. Sometimes a different person can relate where a regular teacher can't. On my notes I complimented the absent teacher on her lesson plan for the day, and to myself chalked that one up to a victory. One student that day made the statement that it didn't matter what they learned, that the other students in school thought they were all dummies. Maybe I overstepped my bounds, but I told him that he had a physical problem and not a mental one. It seemed to sink in, maybe for the first time.

Telling that student I learned my information in college is not entirely true. Being in the classroom and in varying classrooms as a substitute can do nothing if it does not continue your own education. As I've said before, in the school system where I work they send certified substitutes, substitute with teacher certification, into all classrooms. I have sat at one time or the other in all the disciplines. In our society where everyone must specialize, it gives one a different perspective. Perhaps we need positions for generalist, for that is what I think I have become. I've learned things in Home Economics, Vocational Agriculture, and Latin classes that I never would have if I hadn't substituted there. I learned about special techniques in a welding class that I have utilized in my own projects. In shop I learned that a nail driven in with a slight angle is stronger than a nail driven in straight. The list of bits of technical information I have picked up as a substitute teacher goes on and on.

As a writer substitute teaching has provided me with a repertoire of facts and experiences that serve me well. Incidents, such as the time a big girl chased a small boy with a swinging dictionary in her hand gave me a source of real emotional expressions to use later. The big girl had murder in her eyes, the small boy had fear and escape in his. I captured these descriptions and used them with my fictional characters. Verisimilitude is one of the main tools of a writer. The illusion of truth (by the use of many verifiable details) is something I use constantly in my fiction writing.

So this chapter is something that is mostly positive about substitute teaching. Some of the knowledge you gain is earned with headaches and pain in your gut, but those kinds of lessons have a way of sticking. Words are my vehicles and the useful words are sometimes mixed with the obscene ones.

Things have not changed much in that area. Only the obscene words were whispered in my day, now they are sometimes shouted. I don't pay a lot of attention to them. When a boy shouted out an obscene word in class the other day. I did write him out a referral. I don't know if he was calling me one, or someone else. It made little difference to me; I've heard it so many times it's like the word 'stupid.' It's just a word, but still inappropriate to use at times. I was warned about their use of profanity. As a student in education classes they warned us; I just didn't believe at the time the extent I would hear. When it happens it's not nearly as funny. It's taken me years to be able to relegate such talk to such things as frustration and poverty and a desire to express something, anything, with force. I know, no one likes to be referred to with those terms. We learn strong aversion to them early in school. The forbidden words are the words that always impacted us most strongly when growing up. I've used these words, and sometimes still find reason to use them; however, they don't take on the strong emotional implications they once did. As a teacher I know there are many ways to express frustration and anger that are more poignant and effective than the use of these 'bad words,' but these kids are a long way from being able to find the subtle forms of expression that work so much better. So, I let a lot of it go. In the halls especially you hear all the words. If you challenged every cursing student you'd never get to class; you'd be writing so many referrals you'd have chronic writer's cramp. However, you need to draw the line somewhere. The words affect the other students in a different way from the way they affect you. In a classroom, I feel, one needs to maintain some sort of decorum in which all students will feel reasonably comfortable. That is why I wrote up the boy for his obscenity. It's just another word, an ineffective one, to me, but, in thinking about the other students, I decided to do something about this one. You will have to draw your own lines in this area as in so many others.

I think people in general are more tolerant of these words than you would expect. I remember that once in college I spent the night with an aunt who is very religious. My cousin was there and we both talk in our sleep; curse in our sleep his mother told me the next morning. She said my cousin was low and quiet with his, but I rocked the house with mine. She laughed at it.

As a teacher of writing I have seen potential writers use a lot of obscenity. In some cases this is a path toward getting out obscure forms of expression. In some cases, they started with a lot of obscenity but learned, later, better ways to express the same emotions. Many popular books are profuse with gutter language. In a time of my life I found some type of understanding from all that. But today they seem to litter the literary landscape with useless words. Books of the eighteenth century, Samuel Johnson, Alexander Pope, Jonathan Swift, were able to bring to mind bottom dwelling emotions without using the specific profanity we see so much of today, and in that, I think they were superior writers. But that is just my opinion and in my writing I insert occasionally a 'bad word.'

# 14

## *Observation*

You are going to see things. Some of the things you may not want to see. Yet it may be your responsibility to report them, at least make a note to the teacher. You may see things related to drug or alcohol use, or even huffing paint. These things are usually less obvious than you might think. The kids do try to hide them. Before running immediately to the authorities you might want to observe the chain of command and first talk with the teacher in whose class you are subbing. This, in almost all things is the best way to go. Report what you heard, saw, smelled, etc. to a regular teacher. What you do may depend on what it is. Of course, obvious criminal behavior such as threats on the life of someone or something very serious makes it necessary to jump over the chain of command and go directly to the principal; it is his decision as to whether to notify the police, in most cases. You do have that right, but doing so might jeopardize your job, or interfere with an ongoing investigation. Better in most cases to go to the principal first, and if that doesn't satisfy you, go on yourself to the level you think is appropriate. These observations you make in the course of a day might be of a wide variety of things.

You might see a baggy of marijuana fall from a locker. You might intercept a death-threatening note in your classroom. You may observe a bulge in clothing that looks like a gun. Overhearing things that student say, you might believe that rioting is going to take place in protest to something or other. In just about everything that is criminal you may be privy to some information regarding it. But you have to consider that kids say things that just aren't true.

Personally, I hate the idea of informing about anything. Even in areas that are potentially serious I would want to be sure of my observation before mentioning it to anyone. If we become a nation where everyone spies on everyone else then we might become a less attractive nation to live in. However, sometimes, without really trying or wanting to, information appears or comes to us. Hearsay is prevalent, but sometimes, empirical data is before us and we must report it if it puts people at risk. Rarely is it so clear-cut as that. Many times things may be explained in other ways. Communicate with teachers and administration in these cases and decide what is the best course after sharing the information with your peers. Report immediately the serious things, and the others investigate or observe further. Observe and then check out your observations with someone else. If another teacher or two or three think the thing noticed is serious enough, then go to the proper authorities. Again, this is in those situations that are not clear-cut; situations that may not be as they seem at first.

Another thing that may warrant some follow up are the emotional problems you will encounter in your students. It may be the theme some needy student writes. These themes can tear your heart out. A lonely, disenfranchised student, writes of her alienation from others and how she does not have friends or family to talk with. When I see these I write something to the teacher. A note and attaching the theme to my teacher report can get some attention. This can bring something home to the teacher who has overlooked it before. You may see things that the busy regular teacher has not. If I can, I try to give some type of positive attention to the student in question. A touch to the shoulder of a lonely student may have good impact, or a word of praise for almost anything they do or say can help. The student most likely needs to be in some counseling situation or therapy. You can write a note to the counselor, but usually it is best to go through the regular teacher. Many kids these days are in situations like this, and most of them will survive and reach a type of adjustment to their problems on their own. You are not responsible for it, and actually there is little you can do about it. It does pull at heartstrings when one observes it though.

You will see a lot of graffiti. Some of it they will write on the board between classes. Some will be on their clothes and notebooks, but most will be as scribbles on their papers. You don't have to be a psychologist to notice the heavy marks on their papers. These designs may stand out as very angry. The words that are angry may also be written along with cryptic designs. And it is no great leap of logic to assume what the student is feeling. But aren't most adolescents angry at one time or another?

I don't go into my classes with the attitude that I can save the world. Even small things are sometimes above my abilities to change. A little encouragement from me when I can give it, and a note to the regular teacher is the best I can do most times. Maybe you will figure out a better way to do more. There are so many needy kids these days. It would be good if we could do something to meet their needs.

You will see many minor things that might suggest a need for help. One girl turned in a paper. Her handwriting was so small I could barely see it. Such small writing suggests low self-esteem. She probably needs to see someone for some therapy. It didn't seem to be as big a problem, as some, so I only made a short note about it to the regular teacher. Such documentation in passing, as this, may or may not bring results. I suppose most substitutes don't even mention things of this nature. For me though, since I have background in psychology, I feel like I have to at least mention the things I observe. When it's down on paper it's harder to ignore.

There are many things you will observe that need to be reported. In a middle school I saw a boy who was wearing a chain link belt. This boy I knew to be a fighter and with that as a weapon he could have been deadly. I don't know how he had gone so far into the day wearing it without someone seeing and doing something. I reported him, and he lost the belt.

I think the observation of substitutes is of great value. Coming into a class-room with fresh eyes one may see things that go overlooked by those who are there everyday. Sometimes our observations are discounted, but sometimes people listen. I hope you will make these observations and at least write them on your report to your absent teacher. They may help.

# 15

## *Administration*

I have very little direct contact with the administration of the schools where I teach. The principal's secretary is who I report to in the morning and who signs my time sheet in the afternoon. The principals themselves usually have very little to do with the subs. Only when there is a severe discipline problem or when you screw up badly do you talk with the principal. There have been a couple of these times.

In the early days, back in the seventies, I once was subbing in a class full of miscreants. I had one out in the hall talking to him when the principals secretary called me over the intercom, "Mr. Gray, some of your students have crawled out the window and are walking around on the roof." What can you say about that?. They were really slick about it. One would earn a talking-to in the hall as the others crawled through the window and up on the roof. I don't know why I didn't notice my diminishing class that day. I wasn't too with it in that time period.

Another time the principal called me on the carpet. I was in the hall reaming a student out about something as the principal was making an announcement to the school. Somehow my intercom was cutting into the main intercom. While I was in the hall some of my students were pushing the button to the office and they were quietly entering profanity and insults from my classroom into the broadcast of the principal to the entire school. Such is the life of an unlucky sub. I didn't get fired, just criticized and I deserved it then. I've learned that when I talk to a student in the hall, I stand in the doorway so I can keep a look in at the class at the same time.

The principal's secretary is your liaison to the administration at most times. When you report in the morning she will usually give you a class schedule. You need this and would do well to ask for one if she neglects to give you one. School secretaries are different in the way they handle things. Some prefer just to tell you the room number, and others will supply you with everything in writing. In some classes the teacher posts her schedule and its all right. But in some you may be guessing as to what time class starts and ends and especially which lunch to take. In the larger schools they have two lunches. Bells ring and if you go to the wrong lunch your next class may be taking care of themselves for thirty minutes. I've done this and thankfully no disastrous consequences have occurred. I usually ask which lunch, if the secretary does not give me a schedule. It is also helpful to know if you get a planning period.

Subbing is hard when you don't get a planning period off. That extra class may not seem like much to people who are not in the schools, but with me the intensity it takes for just one more class takes a lot out of me. Some people think teachers have it made with just five or six hours of work a day, but let me tell you those are five or six hours that are hard mentally. I've worked ten hours in the oil field and been less tired than from a day in the classroom. Another perk some-times occurs when you get a last hour planning. The secretary lets you go home. The secretary knows the hard days you sometimes put in, and they give you this little incentive to keep you coming back. It is nice to get to go home an hour early. I have had secretaries give me hall duty on these last hour planning's, and it seemed a chincy thing to do, but I do it. Most hall duties are just make-work and to be assigned to it when it doesn't seem necessary makes for a long period. We have a little bit of power in this. The secretaries do need us at times, and they usually treat us well, in ways like this, to keep us coming back. Those who put us on hall duties sometime find themselves coming up short of subs on some busy mornings. And there are some schools where the work is so hard they have trou-ble finding subs to come anytime. My 'bad' school is one where the new subs come and spend only one day, if they make the day. I still go there. Those teach-ers need to be relieved at some times; they need the day off. We have that option of taking a school or refusing it.

In my 'bad' school the students are such behavior problems that subs just avoid it. I probably should. The last time I subbed there I had some out of con-trol classes, and it was a difficult day. My technique while somewhat effective did not get them down to the quietness level I like to maintain in my classroom. Something about the teachers there keeps me going back. They, most of them anyway, work very hard. They have a tough job. They face these behavior prob-lems every day, and they do a good job in spite of the difficulties. I go there because I respect the work they do, or are trying to do, and they respect me for my efforts. In no other school do I have the kind of working relationship as I do with these teachers. In none of my other schools do I feel that my tough job as a sub is appreciated as much as in this school. So, I don't go back there every day, but often enough to feel like I'm doing something for the good of the group.

These are students who need attention, and teachers who need some time off. Hopefully you won't have schools like this in your district. When I needed a reference, the principal there gave me a good one. You may feel that what you do as a substitute teacher is invisible, but it isn't. If your classes go wild all day, which still happens to me at times, someone notices and the word gets out. And, conversely, if you have order in classes that are commonly out of control, someone notices that too. The substitute secretary at this school will sometimes ask me to fill in the hardest classes, and I do, but she gives me some easy days sometimes. I have subbed a couple of time there when I've only worked half days and been paid for full ones. So, it works out.

You will need to see what your tolerances are. I have a friend who only subs in the high schools. She is retired from elementary teaching and the high schools interest her, and are all she wants now. She fills a necessary function and does well at these schools and is happy doing so. Once I talked with a sub who had been in my 'bad' school, and he was simply aghast at the way those students had behaved. I tried to teach him my method for keeping order, but he had been burned too badly. He was looking for anything to get out of the subbing business. Some will have to just get out. I quit a hundred times only to have life's circumstances throw me back to it again. And now I'm glad it did. It has been very rewarding to go into the 'bad' classes and establish, at least, a little order, and to get across some lessons to these kids who really need to learn something.

Some of these middle school kids will grow up by themselves. Something about high school and the unspoken rules among students will straighten some of them out. One can only hope that they have gotten enough of the academic basics in middle school to take them through high school. In some cases the motivation of high school will make them catch up with their peers. Some who I see don't change though. In high school they tend to get lumped together and I see 'bad' classes in high school. These kids are most likely going nowhere. It's easy to give up on them at this level, but I try not to. Even some of these miscreants will wise up later. Some of them will be thrust into the world of work and this certainly has a maturing influence on everyone. Serving up hamburgers day after day will purvey the message better than the discipline at school that learning a little can make their lives easier. And some will come back to school later with different attitudes. I do what I can to get this fact of the unfulfillingness of some jobs across in my classrooms; some listen.

I make my classroom a place of work. I carry enough pencils and paper so that everyone has no excuse for not working. It is a little bit of an expense but how can you expect them to work if they don't have their tools. Yes, they are old enough to provide their own, but some just don't. My theory is to get them used to working and turning in papers, and they will pay more attention to bringing their own tools in the future.

I tell them how it is on the outside world of work. I tell them about operating a metal shear in a factory, wrenching rods in the oil fields, driving a wheat combine on the plains. I let them know about the world of work and some of my descriptions may hit home. I believe that even if you must take some hard jobs in the process of getting an education, it can help. With me these interim jobs were tolerable because I always had the hope of finding something better. Without an education many of these kids can hope for nothing better than menial jobs all their lives. Some become aware of this and learn to try a bit harder. Some can not see past the last bell at school. But even these get several chances. Technical schools are good in my state. With just a little maturity some of the 'miscreants' can learn a skill. A skill can provide the concrete thinking ones a living that is not as hard financially as others. A skill can be the ticket to a better life, but some level of academic understanding, being able to read and understand at a minimal level, is necessary for advance and in succeeding in skilled positions. Mechanics research technical manuals constantly. I try to give some instruction that focuses on the basics so those who will be skilled labor can supplement their knowledge when necessary.

As a sub sometimes you can say things in a different way from the regular teacher that will stimulate them. Some students block on traditional techniques of teaching, and, unconsciously, things register or become clearer when they come from other sources. Sometimes I teach reading or math, in little increments admittedly, that may start them to learning more.

Well, I've gotten way off of my introductory purpose of talking about administration. You, more than likely, will not have much to do with the administration in your schools. If you just focus on your classes the rest will fall into place. If you do have problems with the administration just listen and do what they say. As a sub you have very little bargaining or arguing power. Best to just listen and nod your head and go on. If you feel you have been treated unjustly wait till later and talk with the administrator. Once I wrote a letter to a vice-principal who I thought was wrong in one of his determinations. I didn't expect any results, and didn't get any, but writing the letter did me some good. Your liaison is the substitute secretary. She will take care of you if you have problems. Go to her for advice.

# 16

## *Passing Periods*

Halls seem like precarious places to me. In my day that was where all the fights broke out. Today they seem just as likely to occur in the classrooms but still a number of things (maybe because of the pushing and shoving and running that go on) occur in the halls. I try to stand by my door in the hall during passing periods. For one reason I like to observe these curious beings.

They are weird creatures these children of ours. Their mating habits are constantly changing. In different schools I observed this: some of the couples, instead of walking side by side to their next class now march front to back. Not all of them, but I have seen several. The girl walks in front with the books, the boy with his hands to her waist marches behind. It looks quite odd because they try to get so close that they have to be in perfect step to keep from tripping up. It's a sexual thing for them, I guess, but they look so odd in their march that it is laughable. No more boys carrying books these days.

In middle schools I have caught several boys 'copping feels.' It got bad in one school and I guess my Victorian upbringing rebels at this. I pull the violators I see in and write them up or take them to a principal. Something about just walking the halls in peace seems to be a right to me. Girls, and I would say by far the majority, hate this. It is a violation of their basic rights to privacy, and I think the little miscreants who do this need to be brought to justice. So I watch for this.

You will see all types of absurdities in the hall. Some of the things have been there always: boys puffing up like some species of birds to impress the girls; girls preening themselves and practicing their flirtations on the boys. There must be a doctoral dissertation somewhere on school hallways.

But, in a more practical vein, you need to learn the hallways in your school. First, for evacuation, if that occurs. And then for just finding your way. Some schools have 'A' through 'G' hallways. To find your room number it helps to know the hall it is in. And on that subject I will digress a little bit.

Room numbers are not always as you would think. In some schools they don't follow a logical progression. You may be following what you think is the path to your room to find yourself going outside. Especially in the older schools, some have maze like hallways, you can get lost looking for your room. In one school I found the room number and went in and waited. No students came. I checked and found that there was another room at the other end of the school which had the same number. So I was late. The simplest way to solve this problem is to ask a student. Somehow almost all of them know the rooms by teachers' names. They can direct you to where you need to go.

Another problem is getting into your room. You will find most of them locked in the morning. If your substitute secretary is on the ball it will only be a couple of minutes before the custodian or another teacher opens it for you. However, I have been left waiting with a classroom of students in the hall for someone to open the door. Usually, if it is more than a minute I look for an open classroom, ask the teacher, and call the office to remind them. At times I have sent students to look for a custodian. It can be a problem.

And how they leave the lock can cause some concern. If they leave it so it locks when closed you have to watch it. Once I locked myself out of a class. Students were in the room and I was locked in the hall. They could have had a great deal of fun with me, but, fortunately, one of them let me back in. Leaving the lock so it doesn't lock is a courtesy. You can leave the room on your planning and lunch and get back in. In some rooms, especially computer rooms and sometimes industrial art rooms they want the doors locked when you are out. Expensive equipment could be stolen. In these cases usually the teacher next door can unlock for you. Sometimes, rarely, you will be given a key. Instructions are sometimes given on how to leave the room. I follow these. It could be difficult for you if something important were stolen from a room you covered. Once I chased a boy down the hall to get a remote control back that he had taken. Taking the time to secure a room doesn't cause you much delay and it's best. But if no instructions are left from the teacher I don't worry. In most rooms it is only books that may be stolen, and for some reason you don't have to worry about students stealing books. I guess that is a comment on our society.

In snowy weather you need to watch the halls for snowballs being thrown. This is not so much for the kids as for you. I've been hit a couple of times by snowballs. Thankfully they didn't have rocks in them. However it's a good idea to at least sound off when you see kids throwing them at each other. Sometimes a snowball can lead to a fight and if you can stop it, even a little bit, it might have some good effect. Especially in my climate where it snows rarely this is a problem. The kids get very excited about the snow and lots of horseplay often results.

On a couple of occasions I have seen weapons in the hall. Not guns, but chain belts and knives. You glimpse these sometimes in open lockers. Report them. Only one time did I see what I thought was a gun in a boy's coat. He came into my class and I saw the bulge. I asked him to hand it to me. He refused. I called the principal on the intercom, and in the delay in him getting to the class, and with the commotion of other students entering the room, the boy passed whatever it was off to someone else. When the principal arrived he had nothing. Once I saw a revolver on the principal's secretary's desk, but this is something rare. Even before Columbine not many tried to get guns in the school.

Another new thing in the halls is the scanning machine. Sometimes you may be asked to monitor these, and when I do, I do it with much seriousness. Usually you make adults sign in and then go through the scanner. I look in the women's purses, in all bags, and also feel the book bags for hard objects such as guns or knives. All students are supposed to go through the scanners and I make them. Even if they just stepped outside for a minute I make them go through the scanner again. You may get some who protest but by this time you should be used to student protests and not let them bother you. This is an important duty. I take it seriously and sometimes I make some people unhappy in the way I do it, but it can be, in that one instance, crucial. I saw on the news where in one of the schools where I had manned the scanner before that a boy did get through with a pistol. They caught him later before he caused harm, but he had gotten through the scanner, perhaps with a sub manning it. Some of the scanners, I fear, are not as functional as they should be. This is a relatively new thing in the schools and maybe the technology has to catch up.

Halls are important. My advice is to keep your guard up in the hallways. Many things can happen there that you normally won't see in the classroom.

# 17

## *A typical day*

There are no really typical days as a substitute teacher, maybe that's one reason I enjoy it. It is always something of an adventure. But for an example of what you might expect I will write about one of my days.

In my system they have an automated tapeline. A computer calls you, sometimes a couple of days in advance, sometimes just before the day begins, and tells you your assignment. The school, a job number, teacher's name, subjects, and times are given to you. I write these down and report to the school. High schools start at 7:20, middle schools 8:40. I try to be on time. This helps the substitute secretary set up her day and it helps me get to the classroom and get ready before class starts. Those few minutes to prepare can have a great difference in how your first class and sometimes the whole day goes. I mentioned the 'Bum's Rush' earlier. I think it works. You hit the class with a good assignment just after they sit down, give them a good push, and then little pushes get them through the time block.

Assuming you get into your classroom with no trouble, you find it, and the door is unlocked, the first thing you do is look for posted emergency plans, the evacuation route and bell sounds that alert an emergency. Bell alerts can vary from school to school; one school may use short buzzes for fire and another one a long buzz, so see what your school uses. Plan the evacuation route from the classroom. It only takes a minute and in the event of problems you don't have to worry about this thing. Look the room over and check for obstacles in case of an emergency: blocked doors, TV stands in the way of exits, etc. This done the next thing is the lesson plan.

At times the lesson plans will be left with the substitute secretary or in the teacher's box, but usually they are in the classroom. I prefer a written out sheet on the desk, and this is the usual method, but sometimes the lessons are written on the board. In the clutter of some teacher's classrooms it is sometimes difficult to find them on their desks, and in some cases there are none. Let's say you find the lesson plans on the desk. Go over them. Checking to see if materials such as text-books, overhead projectors, etc. are available. You may want to write the lesson on the board if they are not already there. This saves some time in going over them with the kids; you can just point to the board. It never fails to amaze me how some students can keep from hearing their assignment when you've said it several times. Sometimes you might have to repeat the same thing five or six times. In some cases there will be handout sheets to be passed out. In these the students read and then respond to questions. Check the lesson and try to estimate how much time it will take the class to finish. This is something you will get good at with practice. Some questions take longer than others. Usually about twenty questions will keep them busy for a while, if the questions are somewhat difficult and require research in their books or handouts it will take them longer. If the number of questions seems a little short or too easy (read some of them and answer them yourself) then add some of your own. There may be more questions at the end of the chapter, or you may think of some more. You can just add these to what the teacher has assigned. It doesn't hurt to augment your regular teacher's plans.

I like writing assignments. I think these help the kids in many ways, one of which is the written part of the ACT or SAT test they will take when entering college. Being able to pull information out of their own heads in this unstructured type of assignment makes them think and use skills from all their past studies. It is a simple type of communication, but to be done right the most complex. I try to give as many essay questions as I can.

You don't have to tell the kids you added some questions to their teacher's assignment. They tend to ignore assignments by substitutes. Just give them the extras with their assignment, and don't tell them. Do this for all classes, you may have time to add to the other class assignments later, so concentrate on the first hour first and observe. You may want to modify your assignments to the other classes. There are no hard and fast rules for making assignments so just follow the teacher's plan, and do what works for you. Observe what works for you in your classes. Classes will be different in terms of ability levels, behavior problems, and willingness to work, so you will have to be flexible in your execution of lessons. If you have to, add some more during the class period. Seldom will you need to shorten them.

The kids come in. Look them over. You may be able to predict those who will give you trouble and those you may rely on. Give them the assignment first thing. Well, you probably will have announcements, flag salute, and moment of silence in first hour. You will wait for these. I bet I've said the pledge of allegiance a million times, but I do this for personal reasons and always emphasize the last 'for all.' Some of the kids need to hear this 'for all', I think. Especially in the times we are in now I think it helps some kids, at least, to think about our government and the world situation today. It is a rote thing for most, but some may listen to what they say.

I may or may not go over emergency procedures at first. In case of drills or emergency all that is necessary, if you prepared, is for you to be ready and to assign one student to lead the class. You will need to pull up the rear to make sure they all get out. After being in the classroom with the kids a few minutes you may be able to select a reliable one to lead the kids out, if necessary. In some cases, tornado, (and I am reluctant to even say this) nuclear bomb, the kids will line up in the hall, near the classroom. In some schools they take the 'cover position', squatting and covering their heads. This cover position will usually be done by other students from other classes, so just follow suit. In case of fire or bomb in the school the students will march outside. Don't forget to take your flashlight. It could be very dark going through the halls in such an event.

But back to your typical day. You start a sign in sheet around. Just write sign-in on the top of a page, the period, and the date. Some may sign for others but usually they just sign their own names. If you make sure the signing follows the rows of seats you have a rough seating chart. Just count from the first or back from the last and you may be able to figure out a name to go to one of these faces.

Johnny has drawn your attention. You look at your sign-in sheet and count four back from the last signature and think his name is Johnny, but they were not going in order at the last so you're not sure of his name. He talks loudly to his friends but not disturbing enough to call down yet. The old teacher saying is 'give them enough rope to hang themselves' so you do. The pencil that was thrown across the room seems to have come from him, but you were at the board writing and didn't see for sure. Just wait. And it happens. He sticks his foot out to trip the class untouchable and you see it. The boy falls and his glasses frames are broken again. But the substitutes' problem arises.

"What is your name, son?" I ask.

"My name?"

"Yes, what is your name?"

"You want my school name or one of the others?"

"How many aliases do you go by?"

"What's an alias?"

"What is your name?"

He delays, starts to look around, Almost ignoring me.

"What is your name?" I repeat.

"Bond—James Bond," he finally says defiantly.

I go to the intercom and hold the button down until someone answers, "I have a mister James Bond in my class. I would like for someone to come up and make a positive identification." The office says okay, they'll send someone. By this time Johnny decides to tell me his name. I take the time to write the referral, but first tell the class to get busy on their assignment. If they do and no other problems arise, I have the time to look up all the codes, etc. and write the referral and send Johnny to the office with the person who is coming to identify him. One more James Bond to go for discipline.

Sometimes you may have several problems come up at once. Try to select the most severe and block the others out, as best you can, and stay with the one you started. The others you may be able to do something about later. Many times I've made several go out in the hall together, so I could focus on one behavior problem at a time. This can be a good way to approach several problems at once, because many times someone from the administration will walk by and just take them all off your hands. But in a few cases the administrators want you to tell them why so many students are in the hall and admonish you to write referrals instead of doing this. Do what you can in that situation.

The day goes by. If it is a good assignment and the students are in control, you may not need to use my plus and minus system. But if they don't go immediately to work, you look for the ones who have. You take the sign-in sheet to them and tell them to write a plus by their name. One reason I like this system so well is that you are giving attention and credit to the students who work. Sometimes they are left out in the miasma of behavior problems. They like to give themselves pluses. They don't mind a bit looking up from their work and writing down a plus by their name. I have had classes, so loud I couldn't be heard, suddenly change to library silence when they realize they are being evaluated, and that they can earn themselves something just by being quiet. It is very rewarding when this happens. Not only can I hear myself think, sometimes I can sit down and drink my coffee and relax. After the system has taken effect I tell them they will get two or three pluses for finishing, and sometimes this is all it takes. I can sit back and relax for most of the hour. I usually take the time to look at their papers close to the end of the period. I make some suggestions about grammar, spelling, etc. or complement those who did good jobs, and I give the number of pluses I think they deserve. In most classes I end up giving everyone an 'A' in conduct, based on the number of plusses. It is something that never fails to amaze me.

So your day goes. Sometimes you have a planning to kick back in and sometimes you have to cover another class. Let's say you go to another class and there isn't a sign of a lesson plan. If there are textbooks you ask a student where they are in the book. Find the place in the text, look to the end of the chapter and assign the questions. Or, tell the class to write a summary of the chapter. In low level classes you might tell them to write the first sentence of every paragraph in the chapter as a summary.

I've had this said so many times it echoes. "We've already done this chapter!" It's like they could not possibly do anything they've covered again, and in some, this is just a method for throwing you off.

"You're an expert on chapter seven?" I ask. No answer. "I think we will do it again, and just see if you can find something there you don't already know." Sometimes this works. But let's say there aren't any texts in the room. (sometimes books are checked out to students and none of them bring them to class.)

If there are dictionaries you remember you have some copies of words you made earlier, in your satchel. You have them define words. Say, there is nothing there in terms of dictionaries. You have some simple word puzzles or math sheets you hand out. It won't hurt them to review math even if that isn't the class, but they may rebel and you will have to stick to your guns to get them to do it. But to avoid this conflict, in very rowdy classes, I usually carry a film, "Robin Hood." It has enough action in it to keep some of them distracted. Some may even learn from watching a good film, although this is rare. Most classrooms have access to VCR and TV. This can at least give them something distracting to do while you wait for this class to end.

As I said at first there are no typical days when you sub, but if you prepare a little you can meet almost any challenge. Carry a satchel or book bag and put the things you may need in it for the times when you have to ad lib. I pick up pencils on the floor and carry a notebook of cheap writing paper. It cost very little and for me it is so much better when they all, at least, have the tools to do their assignments.

Again let me stress that many of things that have happened to me in my experience will not happen to you. Sometimes I get bored in the sedate high schools and just go to a middle school for some action. If you approach your days as an adventure they will be.

# 18

## *Abuse by Children*

Charles Dickens wrote about children who jeered and stoned certain adults on the streets of London. I've never been stoned, but I have been hit by basketballs, zinging staples, snowballs, and paper wads. It seems like a singular type of insult. I've felt the particular feeling of lowness at It. —It's not personal. I say that over and over and it's not. These kids will forget you faster than a promise to clean their rooms. You will think about it much longer than they will, and I usually forget it before dinner.

When I was a therapist the problem of insults and what to do about them came up often. In families it is particularly a problem. This is so because in families the members know the weak spots of their relatives. You live with someone and you know how to get at him or her. Sometimes it may be an unconscious knowing, but when arguments erupt and go to the extreme one knows what to say to hurt their family member. In families with alcoholics this is even truer. The alcoholic loses his inhibitions and says things that hurt. I've talked to tearful spouses, son and daughters, mothers, fathers, cousins, and tried to console them and to give them ways to deal with this type of verbal abuse. About the closest, at that time, I could come to helping them was to give an example of a derelict on the street shouting something vulgar at you. In this case one would not react as strongly because the vagrant is nothing to them. I tried to tell people to imagine that the alcoholic family member is not acting as himself or herself, and to just ignore what they say, as they would the derelict on the street. This was not a wholly effective approach. The fact is (I've come to learn) that it always hurts when it comes from a family member.

So, that's where I am now with it. In the classroom when you are insulted (and sometimes it is the insult of being totally ignored by some students) it hooks something inside. You might as well not try to ignore it. Yet, you can learn to not be as bothered or as hurt by it as you may think. You may think the insult is something you can not tolerate, but with practice you can, figuratively, pull the hook out and keep going with just some minor pain. With practice you can not even show the pain of the hook. That is probably best when you just keep on with your lesson and not show that they have said something that cuts. The old saying of water off a duck's back can be applied. It rains on the ducks, you will be insulted, but the rain beads and rolls off. So it can do the same off of you too. Not that the insults happen all the time. With some subs it very rarely occurs, but with me it happens often enough that I feel it and have to deal with it.

There was a time in my career as substitute teacher when I showed my anger. I thought from a selfish standpoint that it was better for me to let it out, not hold it inside. And, I thought it was better for the kids to see what their words and actions could result in. Once I got hit with a zinging staple (they peal a single staple off from a section and hold it on the point of their pencil and flip it). It hit me right under my eye, and I let it out. My voice is strong and they must have heard me all the way down the hall as I yelled at this miscreant who had hit me. As it turned out the principal, whom I respected and liked, was leading a couple of visitors on a tour of the school. He opened my door and just looked at me. It embarrassed me, my yelling outburst, I felt ashamed and I apologized. Now, I try to modulate my anger. I seldom show it at all. And now, I think it is better not to.

Sometimes the kids have to 'fish' to find the hooks that will catch the sub, but they've found them with me at times. In the E.D. class I mentioned earlier I showed a picture of my baby daughter. One asked me how I "got" her, implying all sorts of things. I slammed my fist down on a filing cabinet and dented it. My anger showed blatantly and because it showed the kids kept fishing for ways to bring it out. This was about in the middle part of my time as a sub. I've told you about how they got to me in other ways. This last two years I've been called 'Mr. Gay' a couple of times in the middle schools, but now I don't pay attention to it. Once I asked the boy if he had something against gays. This, for some reason, seemed to stifle him. He seemed embarrassed. Once I told a boy that he must not be very black if he couldn't tell the difference. He erased the 'Mr. Gay' that he had written on the board. Mostly I just ignore it. It seldom happens any more. This is just an example of their fishing. They learned how to hook me at one time and fished that way for a while. They are good at finding the soft underbellies of their substitutes, and I don't think it's just meanness that they do this. It's more like a carryover from their home lives. They bring baggage to class from their homes and they sometimes have a compulsion to carry on the conflicts in class. A substitute is usually a less threatening figure that those in their families, and they think they can get stuff by with him. So, they try.

Again, my advice is to just feel the twinge of pain when they hook you, pull out the hook yourself, and go on. I know it's easier said than done, but it can be done.

You may be scarier than I and can frighten them. I've seen many teachers who can, but that just never worked well for me. Maybe it's my face or something, but I was never successful in scaring these kids. I've had teachers walk in my room and do so with them, but it was never a skill that I got good at. More times than not I would upset the good kids, the kids that come in and sit down and quietly do their work, and the bad kids would not even notice. Some of these kids are really tough to words. And after all, words are all we have anymore. And a sub's words are always less forceful than a regular teacher's. So I found another way to do it.

With few words I set them about to earning pluses for a conduct grade that I can give. The good kids always get credit for doing their work and amazingly the 'bad' kids get caught up in the process, and, in many cases, turn into 'good' kids in my classroom. This is hundreds times more satisfying than blowing off steam and anger at them. To have them quiet and working is rewarding, and cancels out any anger that may have been invoked by their childish comments and words. When I do this I am doing my job. It is not an easy job. No one will tell you that substitute teaching is easy. To do it and do it well (there are few outward rewards that come even from doing it well) is something that you can pat yourself on the back for. Oh, sometimes a principal or another teacher will wander in your room when they all are quiet and working, and you will see the look of disbelief on their face and you know you have done something. Usually your efforts will go unnoticed, unnoticed by everyone but you. And you quickly forget all the insults you have endured because when all the class, and I mean all the class, even the ones who had started out in an insulting manner, turn in a long assignment at the end of the hour, you have won. You have contributed to the education of some children.

It is especially rewarding to pull these papers out of children you know do nothing in class. Sometimes I ignore some insults early on and start giving the same student pluses for very little things: being quiet, opening a book, writing his or her name on their paper. It is sometimes amazing when that same student starts to actually work. Sometimes I count up the pluses at the end of the period and announce the winner. I sometimes give these problem kids some extra ones and to amazement of the whole class(and especially to them) they win with the most pluses in the period. Some, I know, make their only 'A' in their school career in my classes. Even if I cheat a little to make them win I think this might have some odd effect on these, usual, behavior problem kids. It might even carry over into their next class. Who knows?

I said that my efforts usually go unnoticed, but this is really not true. It is impossible for a regular teacher to ignore when all the class turns in an assignment to a sub. You have pulled from them this work that is down in black and white. You have done something and it doesn't go unnoticed.

# 19

## *Last Bell*

Perhaps I have painted too dark a picture of substitute teaching. There are many bright aspects to it. You will be doing something useful and needed. If you are retired it beats sitting at home all day. The students are sometimes fun and amusing. And most of the time it is calm and goes in a fairly predictable way. Sometimes it is boring and you don't mind that either. And another thing to consider is that different people come into it with different levels of skills with people.

I am the first to admit that my people skills are not as good as they might be. Even though I hold a masters in psychology I did not learn early the ways to function well in groups. My early years were fairly isolated on oil field leases in Oklahoma, and my nature is to spend quite a lot of time alone. So you may go into these classrooms possessing more abilities than I may. I think one of the main things, and it seems so simple, is to like the kids. There were times in my teaching career when I didn't like myself very much and that made it difficult for me relate well to the kids. Those were hard days, and I'm glad that now things have changed for me and most of my days as a sub are enjoyable. Some are still hard, but still enjoyable.

Maybe I stressed a little too much the emergency planning for substitutes. It was never stressed to me by the administrations of any of my schools, but those were different times. I don't feel that schools will be number one targets for terrorists. There are lots of people on the lookout at schools which make them difficult targets, even though some say security is lax. It seems to me that many more targets would be easier for terrorists than schools. Now, especially, people have their eyes open, even some students. And when people are alert they pick up on the suspicious activities that terrorist can't help but make. So, hopefully, our schools will be safe and carry on much the same way as in the past. But it doesn't hurt to know emergency signals and evacuation routes. You may be unlucky enough to be in those fractional schools that have an emergency situation. And you will handle it well. Adults take care of business, and you won't be a substitute long if you are not an adult. There are many ways to be effective in emergency situations. You will know your responsibility and carry it out well in your own way.

I hope my technique of using pluses and minuses works for you as well as it has for me. It is a tool and is only as good as the skill of the person using it. If it doesn't pay off right at first give it a little time, modify it, and make it your own in ways that complement your own personality. It is malleable, can be bent into many different shapes and still be effective. Once when I was just thinking about it and didn't have a definite form for it, I just wrote 'Good Student List' on the top of a page and went to the ones in the class who had been working that hour. While it made some impact on this noisy class, its main benefit (and it showed in their willingness to sign) was in getting these good students some recognition. By far, even in the 'bad' schools, most of the students are good. I believe this and I think you will need to believe it if you are to be successful. I believe it about people in general too.

Lots of things may be different from the way I portrayed them. School districts are variable in their approaches to learning. Just be a little flexible and it, on the whole, will boil down to classrooms. They are classrooms like you sat in, even though they have computers in them now, but they still are classrooms. Just classrooms.

'They need to have some order about them for learning to take place, and they need to have a teacher, even a substitute Teacher, to guide the angelical cherubs and the little devils into the ways of knowledge. Maybe you can direct them a little in the ways of wisdom too. If you can, then you've done something. It's hard for me to think of a job that offers more opportunities for doing something good, or more obstacles in doing it. Don't expect any medals, but don't discount it when you overhear in the hall, "That's Mr. Gray; he's a good teacher."

I can dream of a time when substitutes would be looked at as visiting teachers or lecturers. Everyone brings a unique history to the classroom, and they have much in terms of practical experience to offer these students. If we were considered more for what we can bring to these classes instead of just baby sitters, our value would increase. Our status would improve and we would, by necessity, rise to the occasion.

# 20

## *All As One*

This last is a sensitive area in our country. Perhaps I have earned the right to speak about it. I've worked in this inner-city system for several years. Some of the schools are predominantly black, some are predominantly Hispanic, one is mostly Native American, there are representatives from the Asian, Arabic, and white communities in all. All races have been my students. The meanness I have seen came from a sampling of them all, and the goodness, by far the most part, came from all too.

Going from classroom to classroom one thing strikes the substitute teacher. Teachers are all different, different individuals. This is evident from the way they decorate their classrooms. Some classrooms are filled with color, charts and signs. Signs that show sayings or homilies. Things like, "It is not always popular to be different, and being different is not always popular." There are a thousand of these. Read them and get some idea of the frame of reference of the teacher.

My problem is that many of these classrooms seem to be focused on things that separate. I have been in Native American classrooms that show only pictures of Native Americans, and in classrooms that display only black figures from history. These exclusions of other important historical figures seem to be playing up the importance of special interest groups at the expense of many of the important people in our history. In other words some of the divisions in our society seem to be promoted in these classrooms. Of course you can't judge a teacher by what they have hanging on the walls but other evidence supports this.

In the lunchrooms the groups are separate. You can identify the different groups according to race and national origin by looking at their seating in the lunchroom. No, these are not rigid separations. You may see individuals from all groups sitting with others, but the main groups are still identifiable.

Things I see and hear from the students in the classrooms also indicate that racial differences are still active. These comments vary, but they occur and suggest that we are divided in terms of race and national origin to some extent. Also, within the classroom, the like groups usually sit together.

My point is this. In this time of war we need to present a united front. The terror attacks that we may see on our own soil will probably be limited in their effect. They will cause destruction in relatively small, but deadly ways. Psychologically their results may be much greater. The area I worry about being affected is in our racial divisions. Here, I feel, there is the soil for growing conflict in our society. Now more than ever we need to stand as one.

Going back to World War II we see that it was all of us who helped win this war. The Choctaw and Navajo with their unwritten language confounded the German communication lines. The breaking of the Enigma code of the Germans saved countless American lives, and the pioneering work on computers by a man, alleged to be a homosexual, enabled this to happen. There were heroes from all racial groupings in this war, even the Japanese Americans, who were put in camps, formed a fighting division and were honored in their service to this country. Together we were unbeatable. And that spirit, that fusing together as one, is what I feel we need today. We need to put aside our special interests and self-serving beliefs and meet this threat of terror as one.

It can start in the schools. Not necessarily with assemblies and jingo posters on the wall, but with a true coming together in purpose. As teachers, I feel, we need to rally our similarities, present a united front to our attackers and provide and present the cause of our unique system of government to our school children. We can de-emphasize our differences, and pool our resources in resisting this enemy to our way of life. This unity is evident when people believe and act on their commonalities rather than differences.

We need to practice our national motto: E Pluribus Unum—Out of many, One. When our diverse cultural histories come together, united, our main strength as a nation comes to the fore. And then, we will win this war against terror.

0-595-27558-3

Printed in the United States
27618LVS00006B/99

9 780595 275588